At Home in God

At Home in God

Essays from The Way,
1962–1985

Gerard W. Hughes

© *The Way*
First published 2015
by Way Books, Campion Hall,
Oxford OX1 1QS
www.theway.org.uk

All rights reserved.

No part of this publication may be reproduced or transmitted in any form or by any means, electronic or mechanical, including photocopying, recording or any information storage or retrieval system, without prior permission in writing from the publishers.

Cover Design: Peter Brook SJ

Cover photograph © Edinburgh Peace and Justice Centre

British Library Cataloguing-in-Publication Data
A catalogue record for this book is available from the British Library

ISBN 978 0 904717 46 4

Contents

Foreword *by Brendan Callaghan SJ*	vii
Renouncing the World	1
Campus Ministry	10
The First Week and the Formation of Conscience	19
Dying We Live	31
Forgotten Truths of the Spiritual Exercises	44
Jesuit Schools and the Apostolate to the Unbeliever	58
Formation for Freedom	70
Spiritual Development and the Directed Retreat	81
Spiritual Direction and the Priest	96
On Being an Adult in Today's Church	107
Gerard W. Hughes: A Bibliography *by Joseph A. Munitiz SJ and Elizabeth Lock*	117

Foreword

GERARD W. HUGHES SJ is best known for his many books on spirituality, published between 1978 and 2014. But among his first publications were ten articles in *The Way*, the spirituality journal of the British Jesuits, gathered here, in the year after his death, as a tribute to one of the most influential religious writers of the last decades.

'Gerry W.' was born in Scotland in 1924, and educated at Jesuit schools before joining the Society of Jesus in 1942. After his ordination, he was a master at Stonyhurst College for several years, then the university chaplain in Glasgow (where he managed to be sacked twice and reinstated twice by the archbishop), before moving into work in Ignatian spirituality in 1975.

From then until his death he was involved in various ministries concerned with the Spiritual Exercises of St Ignatius: spiritual direction and retreat-giving, the training of spiritual guides and givers of the Exercises, peace retreats, and setting up ecumenical courses in retreat giving and prayer guiding.

His work took him to many parts of the world, including South Africa, Australia, New Zealand, Malaysia, Singapore, Sweden and Finland, and he made two long pilgrimages on foot—one from London to Rome, the other from his Scottish birthplace to Jerusalem.

The period during which 'Gerry W.' wrote for *The Way* spans just 23 years—from 1962 to 1985. The latter date is significant, in that it is the year when the hugely successful *God of Surprises* was first published, following on from his first book, *In Search of a Way* (1978). From then on, Gerry focused on his books, with the last, *Cry of Wonder*, being published only weeks before his death in November 2014.

Many of the key themes of his later writing are present in his *Way* articles: his insistence on a spirituality rooted in the human and in the humanity of Christ; his concern for those who found themselves marginalised in the Church; his engagement with people struggling with belief and unbelief; his alignment with and support for those working for peace and justice in the world; his reluctance to be confined by divisions and boundaries within and among the Christian Churches.

Two brief extracts—from the earliest and the latest of the articles presented here—can serve as examples.

> There is nothing in this world which does not belong to Christ, no human activity which is irrelevant to the Kingdom of Christ. Therefore the work of every Christian in the world has an intrinsic value, and every action, every discovery which contributes to the order, beauty and progress of this world is an act which contributes to the Kingdom of Christ and has an eternal value. ('Renouncing the World', 1962)

> The function of authority in the Church is to help us to grow, to become adult, so that we may become more perceptive and responsive to the mysterious action of God in every detail of our lives, and the action of God is unique to each individual. ('On Being an Adult in Today's Church', 1985)

What is also apparent is the way in which the language used develops to reflect Gerry's commitment to speaking of God's presence and action in our lives in words that were accessible. The slightly heavy earlier style gives way very quickly to the 'everyday language' approach that made his books so accessible.

But reading these essays allows us, above all, to see Gerry developing his ideas, wrestling with his own questions about faith and Church and gospel, finding the ways of writing and speaking that have helped, and continue to help, so many people. It was his willingness to share his struggles that made Gerry such a welcome guide to those of us aware of our own struggles, and makes this collection not just an introduction to Gerry's later books, but a valuable source of insight, guidance and encouragement.

Foreword

If I am to find God in all things, I must find Him within my own self, within its darkness as well as in its light. The most radical ecumenism is ecumenism within our own psyche. It is only in so far as we are able to accept ourselves that we are able to accept others. ('Spiritual Development and the Directed Retreat', 1980)

Brendan Callaghan SJ
Manresa House, Birmingham

A Note on the Text

These essays have been reprinted substantially as they appeared in *The Way* and *The Way Supplement*. A few references to cited works have been added or expanded; occasionally 'this year' or 'last year' has been replaced with a date for clarity; spelling and capitalisation have been made consistent; and a small number of footnotes have been added to explain references to current events at the time of writing. Quotations from the Bible and Ignatian texts are in the original translations used, which may vary. The original publication details are as follows.

'Renouncing the World', *The Way*, 2/1 (January 1962), 44–51.

'Campus Ministry', *The Way Supplement*, 22 (Summer 1974), 78–84.

'The First Week and the Formation of Conscience', *The Way Supplement*, 24 (Spring 1975), 6–14.

'Dying We Live', *The Way*, 16/2 (April 1976), 114–123.

'Forgotten Truths of the Spiritual Exercises', *The Way Supplement*, 27 (Spring 1976), 69–78.

'Jesuit Schools and the Apostolate to the Unbeliever', *The Way Supplement*, 31 (Summer 1977), 47–55.

'Formation for Freedom', *The Way Supplement*, 32 (Autumn 1977), 38–46.

'Spiritual Development and the Directed Retreat', *The Way Supplement*, 38 (Summer 1980), 6–17.

'Spiritual Direction and the Priest', *The Way Supplement*, 47 (Summer 1983), 26–33.

'On Being an Adult in Today's Church', *The Way*, 25/4 (October 1985), 259–266.

Renouncing the World

IN THE RENEWAL OF baptismal vows at the Vigil Service on Holy Saturday, the priest addresses the congregation: 'Now that our Lenten exercises are over, let us renew the promises of Holy Baptism by which we formerly renounced Satan and his works, as well as the world which is at enmity with God'.

Every Christian is bound, if he is to be faithful to his baptism, to renounce the world, because the world is the enemy of God. This renunciation must be complete and continual till the moment of death. By his baptism he receives and recognises Christ; but the world cannot recognise him (John 1:10–13). The Paraclete is sent to him, 'who is to dwell continually with you for ever. It is the life-giving Spirit, for whom the world can find no room.' (John 14:16–17) By his baptism the Christian thus becomes the temple of God and the tabernacle of the Holy Spirit. This transformation takes place in an instant, but we must ratify it throughout our lives. All our growth and all our development must be growth and development into the life of the Trinity. Our Christian life can be thought of as a dialogue with God. He is the first to call us, in baptism, but every thought, word and action of our life will be summed up at the moment of death into our answer to Him. He is always calling and drawing us to Himself; we are always, in everything we do and say and think, answering His call, accepting or rejecting His gift of Himself. If we are to be true to our baptism we must renounce, completely and continually, everything that is opposed to Him. There is nothing in our lives which we can reserve to ourselves. He is a jealous God, and at death He will demand everything so that He can give us everything. Holy scripture makes it clear that we cannot live God's life unless we renounce the world. St Paul tells the Corinthians: 'The world with all its wisdom could not find its way to God' (1 Corinthians 1:21). Our Lord, in his prayer to the Father at the Last Supper, says: 'I have given them

Thy message and the world has nothing but hatred for them, because they do not belong to the world' (John 17:14). St John tells his converts: 'Do not bestow your love in the world and what the world has to offer: the lover of this world has no love of the Father in him' (1 John 2:15). And St James writes: 'Wantons, have you never been told that the world's friendship means enmity with God and the man who would have the world for his friend makes himself God's enemy' (James 4:4).

Many Christians, priests as well as layfolk, tend to feel uneasy when they reflect on the truth that they have chosen God, and that 'the world's friendship means enmity with God'. It would seem to them that there is only one certain way of renouncing the world: literally to leave all things, family, friends and possessions, and to enter religious life. They would find it odd if someone were to say: 'Mr "X" (a well-known politician) has promised to renounce the world, and hopes for high office if his party is returned at the next election'. It is true, of course, that if 'the world' is to be identified with material creation, or with all activity which is not directly concerned with the worship of God, then renouncing the world must mean retiring from this world's activities as far as possible. The Manichees identified 'the world' with material creation, and therefore sanctity, for them, consisted in the greatest possible independence of material things. Matter is evil; spirit is good. It is an easy distinction to grasp and has a specious clarity and attraction for impatient enthusiasts who like to know exactly where they, and the enemy, stand. But the distinction must also deny the reality of the incarnation. For if matter is evil, the Son of God could not have become man. His human body must have been a phantom. Manichaeanism, in its extreme form, did not last for more than two centuries; but it is only an extreme example of the tendency in religious enthusiasts to make a clear distinction between 'spirit' and 'matter' or between 'the natural' and 'the supernatural', and to be quick to label particular things and activities 'material' or 'natural', and therefore bad, and other activities as 'supernatural', and therefore good. The distinctions between spirit and matter, natural and supernatural are, of course, valid and necessary, but it is in their application that errors arise. Even among Christians, 'the world' is too readily identified with all activity not directly concerned with the worship of God; so that what is 'natural' is to be rejected or considered of no value. Prayer, receiving the Sacraments and going to Mass are considered supernatural activities which effect our salvation; working, studying, following a profession, enjoying a holiday are natural actions which are, of themselves, of no value towards our salvation. If a man wants to dedicate his life to God he must, as far as possible, renounce these natural activities and devote himself to the supernatural ones. The world becomes identified in our minds with these natural activities. That is why we feel it contradictory to say, 'Mr "X" has promised to renounce the world and hopes to be in the Cabinet'.

Much of the preaching we hear and the teaching we receive seems to confirm this notion. This life is a vale of tears, a testing place for Heaven. Here we have no abiding city (Hebrews 13:14). We are pilgrims and must not be diverted from our journey to God by the snares and attractions of this world. The Christian must renounce this world and deny himself its passing gratifications if he is to reach Heaven. Human activity, work, pleasure, friendship are of no value in themselves. It is love of God and conformity to His Will which gives life its value. The conscientious Christian who finds himself instinctively drawn to this world, who becomes absorbed in his work and who delights in human friendship, must become troubled and uneasy. He can only be saved if he renounces the world, yet he enjoys it and is attracted by it. Meanwhile his prayer and 'spiritual life' become more and more difficult because divorced from his real life. As the natural side of his life absorbs all his attention he grows estranged from the supernatural. If he is conscientious he may struggle on in this divided state, perhaps trying to salve his conscience by going in for some form of 'Catholic Action' in his spare time and contributing generously to the Church, but he remains troubled. His friends at work seem to get along quite happily without a supernatural life and he will be strongly tempted to follow their example.

The normal advice given to such a man is that he should do all his work in the spirit of the Morning Offering. 'Offer up all your works, joys and sufferings to God. Renew your intention frequently and do everything for His sake in a spirit of penance and love. In this way you remain in the world but not of it. You renounce the world because you do not value it for its own sake but for His sake. Your actions, valueless in themselves, are transformed because they are taken up in the one eternal sacrifice of Christ. Of course God does not need your work, but He does want your love and perseverance in the tasks He gives you. The job you do, the profession you follow, the success you achieve, all these are of no intrinsic value. God will not judge you on these but on the spirit and intention with which you have done them.'

This advice is sound and true in so far as it goes, and can be confirmed from scripture passages, quotations from the Fathers and the Church's decrees. But it still tends to identify the supernatural with particular acts of renewing and purifying intention, and fosters a detached attitude to the world which must lead to apathy about the world's affairs. If it is intention which gives our acts their value, then does it not follow that the less natural interest we have in human affairs, the purer our intention can be, and therefore the more meritorious our actions? Conversely, so long as a man finds a natural delight and joy in his work then it must be difficult for him to act purely out of the love of God. It is always difficult to give a satisfactory answer to non-Catholics when they ask: 'Why are the traditionally Catholic countries the most backward? Why is there (in Britain at any rate) such a dearth of Catholics, apart from converts, prominent in public life? Why are your Catholic schools, with a few exceptions, second-rate in their academic standards?' There are many valid answers to this type of objection. But does not part of the answer lie in the distinction in Catholic minds which limits the supernatural to particular actions directly concerned with the worship of God, while natural actions are considered to have value only in so far as they provide opportunity for supernatural heroics? If 'the world' is identified with non-religious activity, then the Christian dare not become absorbed in his work, for this must draw him away from God. The pagan, on the other hand, can give his undivided attention to the world. The dedicated Communist can throw all his energies into the Party's plans and his attention is not divided by thoughts of an afterlife, nor is he worried by reflections on the intrinsic futility of all he does. His work seems to him to be worthwhile for its own sake. In many of the underdeveloped countries today where the Communists have got to work, the Christian missionaries see their converts deserting them and renouncing their baptism, preferring the natural to the supernatural and this world to God. The process is likely to continue as long as the supernatural is limited to invisible, intangible, spiritual realities divorced from this world.

Is the conscientious Christian who must renounce this world necessarily at a disadvantage in comparison with his pagan neighbour? If we identify this world with human activity which is not directly concerned with the formal worship of God then he must be at a disadvantage. But the distinction between the natural and the supernatural, though valid and necessary in theology, must be carefully handled; for there is, strictly speaking, nothing in our world to which the concept 'natural' can be applied. The whole of creation has been affected by the incarnation. All things are centred on Christ and have their ultimate meaning in him; and every man is called to the vision of God. God need not have created man in this way. He could have left him in a purely natural state; but in fact He did not do so. Even when Adam and Eve sinned, though they lost sanctifying grace, they did not revert to a purely natural state. They lost their supernatural gifts but they were still called to share in God's life. St Paul writes to the Ephesians: 'It was God's loving design, centred in Christ, to give history its fulfilment by resuming everything in him, all that is in Heaven, all that is on earth, summed up in him' (Ephesians 1:9), and to the Colossians, 'Yes, in him all created things took their being, heavenly and earthly, visible and invisible. They were all created through him and in him; he takes precedence over all and in him all subsist.' (Colossians 1:16) In a sense history has ended because God has become man and has risen again from the dead. The union of Godhead and manhood has already taken place once and for all in the person of Christ. And now we wait for Christ's second coming when his victory, already achieved, will be made manifest in the resurrection of the body and transformation of the whole universe.[1] In the meantime it is the duty of every Christian to manifest to the world the justice, mercy and love of God for man, and to bring under the dominion of Christ that portion of the world in which God has placed him, for 'the gospel must be preached all over the world, so that all nations may hear the truth: only after that will the end come' (Matthew 24:14).

It is clear, then, that though we are called to renounce the world, there are forms of renunciation which are thoroughly unchristian. We come to God through our humanity and through the world, not in spite of it, and we shall rise again, not as pure spirits but as human beings. God became man; it is the whole of our nature which is divinised, not some 'part' of our souls only. Therefore to think of 'natural' activities as of no value in themselves, and merely as obstacles to the supernatural life, though they may provide us with opportunities of gaining graces, is to ignore the universal significance of the incarnation. It is to diminish Christ, not to serve him. How is his Kingdom of justice, mercy and truth to be

---

[1] Compare Philippians 4:20–21; Romans 8:19–21.

established in the world if Christians retire from public life as far as possible in the mistaken notion that they cannot serve otherwise, and consider secular pursuits to be of no value in themselves? How can the religious or the priest who is called upon to devote his life to the teaching of mathematics or French literature serve God with true joy and alacrity if he believes that his activity, because it is natural, has no value in itself? He may console himself for a time with thoughts of holy obedience or 'it is not what you do but how you do it'; but he will eventually become an indifferent teacher, or an indifferent religious. It is, of course, true that none of our activity, including spiritual activity, is of any value in itself and apart from God, but this must be properly understood. The Fathers of the Church compared the action of God's grace on man to the action of the sun on plants. Without the sun the plants wither and die, but with the sun they grow and develop to their full stature. So, too, the effect of God's grace on man is to bring him to his full growth and stature. God's grace does not lessen his individuality and freedom, but increases it. His omnipotence does not reduce man to insignificance but raises him up as He raised up Christ. Therefore Christians who are not specially called by God to retire from this world's activities and lead a contemplative life come to Him through their dedication to their work and not in spite of it. Their Mass, reception of the Sacraments and prayer should not divide their attention and make them apathetic about this world's activities, but should, and does in holy people, help them to love and appreciate this world, because they find God in all things and all things draw them to God. The Christian should love and be more attached to this world than the pagan.

What, then, does renouncing the world mean for the Christian? The world which the Christian must renounce is not the material world, not the world of 'natural' activity. Renouncing the world means renouncing that attitude of mind which considers this world to be a closed system from which the Creator is excluded, an attitude which is destructive of the very thing it loves. The maximum of pleasure, or success, or dominion over others becomes the ideal of life; and this is enmity with God. To renounce the world the Christian must renounce idolatry, the worship of a creature, whether it is wealth, or human progress, or sex or the Party programme, which is beneath the dignity of man called to share in the life of God Himself.

It is not easy for the Christian to renounce the world in this way. Indeed it is impossible without that familiarity with God which brings a true sense of dependence on and submission to Him. Without this he will easily delude himself that he is serving God when in fact he is serving the world, and he will be deaf to the promptings of the Holy Spirit. Or he will be tempted to denounce the world as intrinsically evil and to retire from it as far as possible. And those who worship the world will welcome his retirement; for they prefer darkness and the worship of themselves and their own desires or ideas to the worship of God in whom all things subsist. 'We shall be as God and shall recognise no other gods but ourselves' is the cry of the world. 'Thou shalt worship the Lord Thy God, Him only shalt thou serve' is the cry of the Christian. But his cry will be hollow and ineffective unless he gives it meaning by his own dedication to his work, by his thirst for justice and truth in public and private life, and by his love for his fellow men, beginning with his own family; thus showing that belief in Christ is not an obstacle to this world's progress but the condition of it.

By baptism we become 'other Christs'; and the Spirit which raised Jesus from the dead lives in us, too,[2] because we are taken up into the life of the Trinity. But we can only grow in the Divine life in proportion as we die to ourselves and give ourselves completely to God, for the life of the Trinity is a life of giving. There is nothing which the Father has which is not wholly the Son's and Holy Spirit's,

---

[2] See Romans 8:11.

nothing which the Son has which is not wholly the Father's and Holy Spirit's. If we are to live the life of the Trinity, ratifying our baptism, then there must be nothing in our lives which we do not give to the Father. At the moment of death He will demand everything from us. Each Mass in which we offer the whole of our lives to the Father in the death of Christ, is a rehearsal for the moment of our own death. But every moment and every action of our life makes up the content of our offering, and the content is different for each one, for each has a different function in the Body of Christ. There is nothing in this world which does not belong to Christ, no human activity which is irrelevant to the Kingdom of Christ. Therefore the work of every Christian in the world has an *intrinsic* value; and every action, every discovery which contributes to the order, beauty and progress of this world is an act which contributes to the Kingdom of Christ and has an eternal value. 'The deeds which they did in life go with them now.' (Revelation 13:14) However, the Christian dedicates himself to the world, trusting in God, not in his own ideas of progress. God may seem to destroy our efforts and to break us as Christ was broken on the cross. But it is in our weakness that God manifests His power,[3] and it is only when we have given everything to Him that He will raise us to life again. Therefore, as Christians, our standards in all our work must be higher, our dedication to work and to the interests of our fellow men must be greater than that of the pagan, for it is in this way that we give ourselves to God and form our answer to His call to us in baptism.

---

[3] 2 Corinthians 12:8.

Campus Ministry

THE TELEPHONE RANG at the Samaritans' office when I was on duty. It was a woman's voice, distressed at her eight-year-old son's refusal to do his homework. We discussed schools and eight-year-olds. 'You seem to be interested in education. Are you a teacher?', she asked.

In this article I shall describe chaplaincy work as I experience it, and leave the reader to answer the worried lady's question.

What is the role of a university chaplain? The question brings back memories of interdenominational chaplains' conferences, where the questions, and the answers, recur with monotonous regularity. One answer, which I shall always remember, came from a hearty English chaplain, 'to get to know the chaps'. 'But how?', asked a timid newcomer. 'In the student bar, old man, where else?', was the reply. Then the discussion develops with quotations from Bonhoeffer, Harvey Cox and John T. Robinson, the Catholics throwing in bits of Rahner, Küng and Schillebeeckx. If the beer flows freely enough, we move on to every aspect not only of university life, or even national life, but of cosmic existence. Then we return to the earthy reality of our own chaplaincies and get on with the real work of emptying ash trays and clearing up the mess after last night's party, hearing for the thousandth time that the Vatican is far too wealthy, being asked why desiccated celibates should tell the laity how to think about sex, and what is the point of going to Mass anyhow? The questions may bore us, but at least the questioners are interested enough to come and ask. In my experience, the vast majority of students coming up to university from their Catholic schools arrive with the firm determination to keep as much distance between themselves and things Catholic as is compatible with their eternal salvation. In simpler language, they come to fulfil their Mass obligation but have little interest in studying the implications of the action they perform. They were given all the answers at school before they could formulate the questions, and they were not impressed. If some do begin to show interest, there is always the danger that they form an elite, which becomes an effective deterrent to the rest of the student body. And if the chaplain does succeed in keeping the chaplaincy out of the hands of a clique and makes it a welcoming place, an area of freedom within the university where students are encouraged to think through their faith and express their own opinions without fear of condemnation, are allowed to exercise initiative, to enjoy the liturgy and contribute to it, is he not then liable to fall into the greatest danger of all? If the centre answers the needs of today's students, does it not inevitably intensify their irritation with the institutional Church as they know it, and unfit them for a return to their own parishes, thereby annoying the local clergy, including, possibly, the bishop, and cause the unfortunate chaplain to be branded a dissident and rebellious priest? Students, of course, will love this, and will give enthusiastic support to the chaplain to lead the revolution. This is the situation in which many chaplains find themselves; many excellent men have hurled themselves against the ecclesiastical barricades, ending up bruised, battered and disillusioned with the Church, eventually resigning to become married social workers. When the storm is over, those Catholic students who never came near the chaplaincy survey the wreckage and are confirmed in their apathy; and the enthusiastic students, who were helped by the chaplain and supported him, share his disillusionment and withdraw from the institutional Church, while the more conservative clergy and bishops congratulate themselves on their unyielding defence of the faith.

If a university is doing its job, it should be encouraging its students to sharpen their powers of observation and criticism, and teaching them to think for themselves. If the chaplaincy is doing its job, it should be helping the students and staff to apply those same powers of observation and criticism to their faith which, if it is genuine, must seek understanding. A student who has benefited from this kind of education is disinclined to accept any authority, whether sacred or secular, merely because it bears the label 'authority'. This is not the same as rejecting authority. He respects and will accept the authority of competence. Unless a university chaplain can share this attitude, he will be pastorally ineffective: if he does share it, he is almost certain to be suspected by ecclesiastical authority, because the spirit of questioning has not been encouraged in recent centuries in the Church. The local church often panics in the face of criticism. One Catholic journalist headed an article, largely devoted to an attack on a university chaplain, 'Satan's Smoke Curls through Cracks in Peter's Barque'.

The university chaplain in this situation is liable to get hurt. He may be the type who thirsts for martyrdom but, if so, he should suspect his motives. There is a false thirst for martyrdom which may spring from a masochistic streak in character, or from simple vainglory. I think that martyrdom for today's university chaplains is slow, painful and inglorious. It consists in listening and entering into the minds of the university community and trying to communicate their thoughts patiently, clearly and persistently to the hierarchy. If the chaplain cannot listen, he cannot teach either.

For most chaplains I do not think it is a question of deliberately rocking the boat: the boat rocks. Almost daily one meets the same problems, perhaps best illustrated by quotations from students themselves. Recently the student president of the Glasgow University Union told me, 'to me and most of my contemporaries, Christianity means nothing'. Subsequent conversation revealed, as it so often does, that by Christianity he meant pharisaism in the Church. There are so many engaged couples who say, 'we don't intend bringing up our children as Catholics, but as Christians. We don't want them to suffer the indoctrination we had.' Then there are the students, full of idealism, who say, 'Yes, I thought about the priesthood when I was younger, but I see it as totally irrelevant in today's world'. 'What do you really want to do?', I asked one student, who gave the shattering reply, 'to burn down churches': an extreme example of so many worried, scrupulous, Catholic students for whom religion is a code of morals to be observed under pain of mortal sin and eternal damnation, which they have the sensitivity to imagine but feel helpless to avoid. In general, I find that the more intelligent and religiously committed students are, the more critical they are of the Church as they experience it.

It is against this background that I want to laugh, or cry, or just groan when I hear the pronouncements of some of our bishops and read the Catholic press. 'Reassertion of Infallibility Doctrine'. 'Reassertion of *Humanae vitae*'. 'No Communion before Confession'. Yes, these questions have their importance, but in the present state of the Church, fussing about them is like rearranging the deckchairs on the *Titanic*. I used to be very interested in dogma: I am even more interested in it now, but in a different way, having spent some years listening to people talk of their understanding of doctrinal and moral teaching, and observing the huge gulf between the theologians' world and that of the people of God. For most Catholics whom I meet, infallibility, for example, is of no importance whatever; or, if it is important to them, it has stifled any spirit of inquiry and verges on idolatry. As for the confession before communion question, the present student generation, which was introduced to confession before communion, is no longer interested in either; and I have met more people who have lapsed because of their confessional experiences than from any other single cause.

University chaplains must try to communicate this experience, not only to inform the bishops, but also to correct distortions in their own perception of what is happening. Every university chaplain, whether he likes it or not, is a theologian, because his theology is expressed in his behaviour, in his priorities. If he is a bad theologian his action will be heretical, an 'unorthopraxis', and tear the local church apart. As chaplains we tend to seize upon the social dimension of the gospel and emphasize the active pursuit of social justice as a primary duty of every Christian. The danger is that we emphasize it to the exclusion of another equally important truth: unity within the local church. Enthusiasm for social justice can so easily degenerate into a glowing love of humanity and a contempt for anyone who does not share our vision and indignation at the world's and the Church's injustices. I heard this thought crudely expressed at a very crowded Midnight Mass, where the congregation was mostly students. At the Prayer of the Faithful one youth, leaning nonchalantly against the back wall, broke into spontaneous prayer. 'Lord', he said, 'Some of us can't stand the bums who hang around George Square [where there was a soup kitchen for the homeless] and others of us can't stand the archbishop. Lord, help us to love both.'

How are chaplains to communicate their experience to the Church and, in particular, to the hierarchy? I think this is an important part of the chaplain's role as teacher—giving expression to the mind of the Church within the university. It is important, because university people do not speak simply for themselves. They also express, but usually more articulately, thoughts and attitudes which are widespread in the Church. University chaplaincies are useful listening posts within the Church for learning the mind of the Church. That is why bishops should be particularly interested in them if they are to learn of the pastoral needs of their people.

One level of communication is through chaplains' conferences. In Britain I think that our annual conferences fail through inadequate preparation. Tired men gather. A few theologians may be brought along to give us the latest on christology or theology of the Eucharist. Gentle snores. We want to relax, not anguish over problems or attempt to articulate our experiences and present them clearly to the Church. There is a final business session, usually about money. I long to attend a well-prepared meeting in which one or two aspects of chaplaincy work are carefully written and circulated well beforehand, so that discussion in small groups can begin at once, draft proposals be produced, prayed about in common, and brief recommendations demanding answers sent, together with background documents, to the hierarchy.

There are eight universities in Scotland, and the Catholic chaplains have a one-day meeting every term. In the last five meetings we have invited the bishop in whose diocese we meet to join us. They have all accepted the invitation, attending for at least half the day, and have shown interest. Although some have found the experience depressing and others bewildering, I think these meetings have helped towards a better mutual understanding.

In Glasgow, as a result of a dismissal by the archbishop followed by a reprieve, I now have a group, rather grandly called 'The Chaplaincy Commission', chaired by the auxiliary bishop of Glasgow and including two university professors, two lecturers, a Catholic headmaster, a parish priest and a student. The function of this commission is to help and advise the chaplain in his relations with other public bodies in the university and city, especially in relations with the local church. The commission is a most useful body, with which I can discuss chaplaincy questions openly, and I am helped by their advice and supported with their cooperation. I think the bishop also finds it a useful experience, exposing him to the university's ways of thinking, which are often so different from the hierarchy's, and showing him aspects of chaplaincy work which may not have occurred to him before. I also have the equivalent of a parish council, composed largely of students, but with two members of staff, and two other members who do not belong to the university but attend the chaplaincy regularly.

Another area in which the chaplain can learn and teach is in relations between parents and students. This is obviously easier in a university like Glasgow, which draws the majority of the students from the immediate area and where 70 per cent of the students live at home. With many of these students one of the most common sources of strain is not study, finance, sex or drugs, but conflict with parents. Every year I invite the parents of first-year students, in batches of 150 at a time, to a social evening. It begins with Mass, with the students preparing the liturgy, followed by a buffet supper, which students prepare and serve. In the course of the evening I tell parents about the work of the university and chaplaincy, and leave them plenty of time to ask questions and discuss among themselves. These evenings can sometimes dispel the fears of parents, especially those who have not attended university themselves, and can lessen conflict at home. Later in the year I put on a special course of lectures, specifically designed to bring the generations together and inviting outside speakers. This year the course of four lectures had an average attendance of 140 at each lecture.

Another example of the teaching role of the chaplain in which the chaplain does not do the teaching is the Glasgow Medical Group. Since 1968 I have been organizing a course in medical ethics for Catholic students in fourth- and fifth-year medicine. In the first year I gave the course on my own. It was very inadequate. Thereafter, I brought in a team of Catholic doctors and consultants to speak on ethical questions in their own field, limiting myself to a brief introduction. In the last two years I have advertised the course more widely and invited some non-Catholic consultants. Attendance has increased among the other denominations and interested agnostics, but Catholic students still tend to keep away. I then heard about the London Medical Group and saw its annual programme, an impressive list of weekly lectures and seminars given by well-known medical consultants, lawyers, philosophers and theologians on some of the ethical questions which arise from the practice of medicine. Average attendance at the London lectures was a hundred. I wrote to the director, Fr Edward Shorter, an Anglican priest, and invited him up to Glasgow. We now have a Glasgow Medical Group, which drew over 200 to its last meeting, held in a lecture hall which normally holds 140. I found that watching Edward Shorter operating was a most useful lesson in chaplaincy work. He took great care in explaining the project to students, emphasizing that its success was in their hands. He took even greater care in approaching members of the medical faculty, to ensure that the organization did not fall into the hands of any particular Christian denomination or any particular medical school. Very shortly, the students will meet to draw up a list of lecture and seminar topics for 1974–1975. This will be submitted a few weeks later to a panel of medical and other university faculties (law, philosophy, theology, sociology), who will advise on lecturers. I am acting as secretary until the organization is under way. I can see possibilities for work of this kind in other areas — education, law, the social sciences — in which the chaplain is not so much a teacher as a catalyst for teaching.

What about formal teaching? The main opportunity I have for formal teaching is through the liturgy. I am uncertain about many aspects of chaplaincy work, but on one point I am very certain. Attractive presentation of the liturgy is the top priority. The homily at Mass, one or two minutes on weekdays and ten to fifteen minutes on Sundays and holy days, is the only regular opportunity for teaching students in large numbers. In preparing homilies I try to study biblical commentaries, but I consider listening to students is just as important, so that the homily speaks to the questions they are asking.

In the chaplaincy I try to put on a course of seven theology lectures on a weekday evening in the first term, giving some myself and also inviting other speakers. Attendance varies from forty to twenty. On most Sunday evenings during term, when attendance varies between seventy and twenty, we have a speaker on some theological topic. We also have discussion groups. During term we have six groups, with about eight in each group, meeting on weekday evenings for an hour. Sometimes these groups are successful and continue for the first two terms, often they fizzle out before the end of the first term. So much depends on the subject they choose, but above all on the composition of the group. If the members of the group can listen to each other, they do learn quickly, because they learn to see with another person's mind truths which had never occurred to them before. In universities, so many students suffer from mental indigestion, their minds sated with information which they have no desire to assimilate. This stifles their curiosity and leaves them in a state of mental apathy. In such a state there is little point in offering them more theology lectures, but if they can be inveigled into a discussion group and persuaded to take an active part in it, they sometimes recover their appetite for learning. I have come to think that religious teaching at university for the average student should not be primarily to provide information but to enable them to develop attitudes and ways of seeing life, which help them to understand what religious language is talking about. I think I teach as a chaplain not by providing information but by helping to create the conditions in which they can learn. Every year I take away a group of 35 students, mostly first-year, for five days in the Highlands. Living conditions are austere, they cook for themselves, have two formal discussion sessions in the day, but no lectures. They prepare the liturgy each day. Thrown together in these conditions, they learn quickly from each other, experience the joy of living for a short period in a community which worships and works and enjoys itself together.

Most chaplains do not have the time to give formal teaching themselves, but I think all chaplains must be teachers in so far as they try to help in creating the conditions in which the university community can learn.

The First Week and the Formation of Conscience

THE PHILOSOPHERS tell us that conscience is not a mysterious little inner voice: it is our human intellect applied to our human behaviour, the mind of man making moral judgments, the dictate of right reason. But these definitions do not begin to describe conscience as we experience it, its power to shake and disturb, to comfort and reassure, its mysterious, imperious quality.

The Old Testament did not have a word for conscience. Instead the writers use 'the heart', 'the reins' and so on. Conscience denotes that core of human sensitivity where body and spirit are at one, and 'gut' reaction, not merely an intellectual judgment. Reaction to what? Reaction to something which is both within us and beyond us. God is not our conscience, but He speaks to us in the depths of ourselves. 'The word of God can slip through the place where the soul is divided from the spirit—it can judge the secret emotions and thoughts.' (Hebrews 4:12) In Romans, St Paul seems to use faith and conscience as synonymous. 'Hold on to your own belief, as between yourself and God—and consider the man fortunate who can make his decision without going against conscience.' (Romans 14:28)

Whatever an adequate description of conscience may be, formation of conscience must, from the very meaning of the word, include growth in self-knowledge, which is not the same as intellectual knowledge about ourselves, but includes a developing knowledge of our own emotions and feelings. The greater the unity and integrity of our being, the more sensitive conscience will be. The saints were alarmingly conscious of their sinfulness. Therefore, formation of conscience includes growth in self-knowledge and a growing harmony and integrity within ourselves. In Christian teaching, growth in self-knowledge and integrity is not possible through individual effort. Man is a related being. 'Before I formed you in the womb I knew you; before you came to birth I consecrated you.' (Jeremiah 1:5) 'You have created me for yourself, and my heart is restless until it rests in you.'[1] It is only in so far as a man looks beyond himself, opens himself to the transcendent God, that he can know himself and find unity within himself.

St Ignatius, in the introductory observations to the *Spiritual Exercises*, writes: 'We call Spiritual Exercises every way of preparing and disposing the soul to rid itself of all inordinate attachments, and after their removal, of seeking and finding the will of God'.[2] The *Exercises* were written in the sixteenth century. Can they help twentieth-century man, living in a very different world, to rid himself of those attachments which prevent him from finding God's will? An insensitive, unformed or deformed conscience blinds and deafens us to God's will. If the Exercises are to help in the formation of conscience, they must lead us to self-knowledge, open us up to the transcendent God and so develop in us a harmony and integrity of our whole being. Can they do this for modern man? Before I attempt an answer, I should like to meander through my own experience.

Certainly, we need help more than ever today in the formation of our conscience. I work as chaplain to Catholics at Glasgow University. Frequently, students say, 'I haven't been to confession for years. I feel the need to go but think this may only be the effect of years of indoctrination in a Catholic school. Besides, I don't know what to confess. I'm not sure what sin means any more. I no longer believe the moral teaching I was given and don't know what criteria to apply to my own behaviour.' Others complain of feeling trapped. 'The Church tells us that we are free to follow our conscience. She also tells us that our conscience is false if it does not

---

[1] Augustine, *Confessions*, 1.1.
[2] *The Spiritual Exercises of St Ignatius*, edited and translated by Luis J. Puhl (Chicago: Loyola UP, 1951), n. 1 (hereafter cited as Exx).

agree with Catholic teaching. Rome and the Kremlin offer the same kind of freedom: the freedom of conformity.' I was in a group of students recently and we were asked to give an adjective to describe ourselves. Five out of eight gave 'confused'. The confusion is not limited to students. I have met many parents who have admitted to greater confusion than their children. Their children can cope more easily with change and uncertainty than they, who were brought up in a much more rigid Church in which questioning was discouraged. The confusion is not, of course, limited to the Catholic population. Universities are full of very knowledgeable people, but the academic specialist can be a helpless fool in his personal life and relations. In our educational system we have divinised the intellect and brutalised the emotions. This has enabled us to make rapid progress in technology and acquire vast wealth. We possess the means to the good life, but we cannot live well. The century of technological progress has also been the century of ingenious torture, subtle manipulation of human beings to serve the needs of the economy, and of mass extermination. In Britain, the issue in the last two national elections has been economics, not human health. 'By yon bonnie banks and yon bonnie braes of Loch Lomond' lies the highest concentration of nuclear weapons in Europe. The emotions have been so successfully deadened that we no longer realise that we are acting inhumanly, we no longer know who we are. I hear so many say, 'I feel I'm being processed. I no longer know who I am.'

I suggest that there are three factors which contribute to the confusion I have described—a predominance of fear, a distrust of self, a tendency to over-conceptualise. These three factors inhibit the formation of a Christian conscience. In Ignatian language they can be called 'inordinate attachments'.

Fear

An Anglican woman was interested in learning more about the Roman Catholic Church. In general she was attracted, but some aspects repelled her. One dislike was the Catholic habit of calling some feast days 'holidays of obligation'. Her first experience of a holiday of obligation after becoming a Roman Catholic confirmed her distaste. In the bench beside her, a mother of two restless children leaned over and told them, 'If you don't attend this Mass you'll go to hell'. Imagine that, as a small child, your parents take you along to meet good old Uncle George. They tell you that he is very rich, very wise, very powerful, very loving and he can give you everything you could wish for in life. You meet Uncle George in his forbidding mansion. He tells you that he wants to see you every Sunday for forty minutes for the rest of your life. 'If you don't come', he says, 'come on and I'll show you what will happen'. He leads you down a dark and stinking passage to a vast furnace room, opens the door of one. You hear the screams, see the horror, smell the burning flesh of children. On the way home your parents ask, 'Do you love Uncle George more than anyone or anything else in the world?' 'Oh yes', you answer, 'with all my heart and soul and strength'. You loathe him as a hideous monster, but you dare not admit it, even to yourself. The all-merciful and loving God has put us in this vale of tears, which he has peppered with landmines, and if we put a foot wrong by committing one of the many acts labelled 'mortal sin', then we spend an eternity in hell. Mortal sin includes missing Mass on Sundays and any deliberate pleasure in sex outside marriage. This fear is crippling. It stifles knowledge of God's revelation and makes a mockery of the gospel. It makes people afraid to think for themselves, in case thought leads them astray. This, together with a natural mental inertia, ensures a lasting disinterest in religion. Fear of sexuality makes us afraid of ourselves, of our own feelings and emotions which are the motive forces of our life, cuts us off from others and so renders the greatest of commandments an impossibility for us. The predominance of fear cripples conscience.

Self-Distrust

As Catholics we are encouraged in self-distrust. By original sin we are wounded in mind and will, and our emotions have run riot (concupiscence). Since we can trust neither our mind, nor will, nor emotions, the only wise thing to do (but how can we trust our judgment on this?) is to put our trust in something or someone outside ourselves, for example in the Church, or in some other system or person who can promise us security convincingly enough. Is this why there is such bewilderment and confusion among so many Catholics at change in the Church? Does this self-distrust explain the readiness of some Catholics to become Communists and some Communists to become Catholics, exchanging one authoritative system for another? Where there is no self-trust, there can be no growth in self-knowledge, and therefore no development of conscience. Self-distrust cripples human development.

Over-Conceptualisation

We have divinised the intellect and consigned the emotions to the animal in us. I heard a story of a baby in hospital who was not responding to treatment. The consultant summoned the nurse, told her to care for the baby as though it were her own, but added, 'Don't tell anyone I said this'. The child recovered, but because the method was 'unscientific', the consultant was ashamed of it. Emotions cannot be measured, quantified, and so they are discounted. Yet emotions, from the very meaning of the word, are the motive forces of life. Stifle them and you stifle life. 'But they are dangerous.' Of course they are dangerous, especially when stifled. 'But they must be controlled by reason.' Yes, of course they must, but by the reason that is in them; and so to control them we must know them. I read of an experiment conducted with small children. They were provided with all kinds of food and no restraint was put on them. After a short period they were selecting a balanced diet for themselves. They had not studied dietetics but their feelings, no doubt unpleasant, had taught them to eat reasonably. There is not time to elaborate this point. If the feelings and emotions are not respected, if they are ignored and treated as the slaves of reason, then they take their revenge in insensitivity, sentimentality or debauchery.

Over-conceptualisation affects us all, irrespective of our religious belief or lack of it. Fear and self-distrust can afflict Catholics more than others. When all three are combined, it is not surprising that we find a Catholic population which tends to be passive, responding only to given stimuli (for example, the Catholic schools and abortion issues), showing no great initiatives, a lack of enthusiasm except when we start tearing each other to pieces in the interest of 'orthodoxy', a ready acceptance of a clerically dominated Church, which assures us of our eternal security provided we do what we are told. Hence the frequent appeals from hierarchy and clergy for greater loyalty and obedience, and the shrill condemnations of all who seem to rock the boat. As we distrust our emotions, we can become capable of acting inhumanly in the name of God. I'm sure that many of us could write a book of horror stories illustrating Lucretius' thundering lines: *Tantum religio potuit suadere maloram*—such evil deeds could religion prompt.

* * *

How far does the First Week of the Exercises hinder the formation of conscience?

James Joyce's account, in *Portrait of the Artist*, of a Jesuit retreat is a classic accusation of the Exercises as instruments of fear. St Ignatius must not be blamed for the ferocious and sadistic exuberance of some of his sons; but the Exercises themselves do seem to instil fear, to encourage self-distrust and to be over-conceptual. Here are some examples taken from the text:

The First Week and the Formation of Conscience

Fear

The petition of the first exercise:

> Here it will be to ask for shame and confusion because I see how many have been lost on account of a single mortal sin. (Exx 48)
>
> I will consider that they [the fallen angels] went to hell for one sin .... (Exx 50)
>
> By their sin they [Adam and Eve] lost original justice ....
>
> On account of this sin ... great corruption ... came upon the human race that caused many to be lost in hell. (Exx 51)
>
> [Consider] one who went to hell because of one mortal sin .... Use the understanding to consider that because of sin, and of acting against the Infinite Goodness, one is justly condemned for ever. (Exx 52)

The hell meditation:

> To see in imagination the vast fires, and the souls enclosed, as it were, in bodies of fire. To hear the wailing, the howling .... [To smell] the filth and corruption. To taste the bitterness of tears, sadness and remorse of conscience. [Consider] those who were lost before the coming of Christ; those who were lost during His lifetime; those who were lost after His life here on earth. Thereupon I will give thanks to God our Lord .... (Exx 65–71)

Distrust of Self

> I will consider myself as a source of corruption and contagion from which has issued countless sins and evils and most offensive poison. (Exx 58)
>
> How is it that the earth did not open to swallow me up, and create new hells in which I should be tormented for ever? (Exx 60)

Over-Conceptualisation

The First Principle and Foundation, which prefaces the *Exercises*, is a masterly piece of abstraction.

> Man is created to praise, reverence and serve God our Lord, and by this means to save his soul. Everything else, which must include persons, is a means to help me to this end; therefore I must use them in so far as they are helpful, rid myself of them in so far as they hinder me.

What potential dangers there are in this First Principle! The danger of seeing everything and everyone as a means to an end, encouraging blindness and insensitivity. The end is presented as 'the salvation of his soul'. Individualism is the death of religion and a desire to improve our own lives can be just as self-interested as any other form of egocentricity.

※ ※ ※

The Exercises seem more calculated to distort conscience than to form it, to stifle it rather than give it growth. They can produce conformists, not men of initiative and originality. They can produce soldiers — theirs not to reason why — papal shock troops, whose hallmark is loyalty and obedience to orders from superiors, unloving and unloved men. Jesuits are often accused of having such characteristics. But the early Jesuits and many, thank God, today, cannot be accused of being frightened conformists, fearful, distrustful of themselves and atrophied in their emotions and feelings. The early Jesuits were exciting men of vision and initiative, and they attributed their spirit to the Spiritual Exercises. What has happened? Were they altogether different breeds of men, or were the Exercises given differently in the early Society? The Exercises were certainly given differently in the early Society and we are only now returning to the original method by giving 'directed' rather than 'preached' retreats. An adequate answer to the objections I have given to the First Week of the Exercises would require a further article, which I hope to write later. Here I can mention only a few points.

How far do the Exercises help in the formation of Christian conscience?

We can, in Christian teaching, only come to self-knowledge and find unity within ourselves, which are both essential if conscience is to be sensitive, in so far as we turn towards God. The preparatory prayer of every exercise in the First Week is: 'I will beg God our Lord for the grace that all my intentions, actions and operations may be directed purely to the praise and service of His Divine Majesty'. Their object is to help us seek and find the will of God, to find all things in Him and God in all things, dwelling in them, labouring in them, source of all that is good, merciful and just. The Exercises certainly encourage us to turn away from ourselves towards God. But what kind of God do they present? Do they use the concept of God to force us into a ready-made pattern of behaviour, to make us conformists?

The Exercises certainly do not encourage a conformist mentality. The whole object is to help the exercitant to discern what is God's will for him or her. They are exercises in sensitivity of the whole person before God and they pay particular attention to the emotions and feelings of the individual exercitant, so much so that Ignatius never gave the Exercises to groups, but always gave them individually. The Exercises fail and can be very dangerous when we attempt mass production, preaching them to large numbers. A few quotations from Ignatius' preliminary observations, later called Annotations, illustrate his delicacy and sensitivity:

> The one who explains to another the method and order of meditating and contemplating should narrate accurately the facts of the contemplation or meditation. Let him adhere to the points, and add only a short or summary explanation. The reason for this is that when one in meditating takes the solid foundation of facts, and goes over it and reflects on it

> for himself, he may find something that makes them a little clearer or better understood .... Now this produces greater spiritual relish and fruit than if the one giving the Exercises had explained and developed the meaning at great length. For it is not much knowledge that fills and satisfies the soul, but the intimate understanding and relish of the truth. (Exx 2)

If that Annotation were understood and observed, most of the objections I made earlier would not stand. Incidentally, what a revolution there could have been in education if Jesuits had always followed the spirit of this observation in their schools.

The Fourth, Ninth and Eighteenth Annotations warn the director to allow the exercitant to go at his own pace, caution him against giving anything too advanced or too subtle:

> Each one should be given those exercises that would be more helpful and profitable according to his willingness to dispose himself for them. (Exx 18)

> The director of the Exercises, as a balance at equilibrium, without leaning to one side or the other, should permit the Creator to deal directly with the creature, and the creature directly with his Creator and Lord. (Exx 15)

> [The director] should not seek to know the private thoughts and sins of the exercitant. (Exx 17)

> If the director observes that the exercitant is in desolation and tempted, let him not deal severely and harshly with him, but kindly and gently. (Exx 7)

It is a pity that St Ignatius did not give the retreat to James Joyce! But how does the exercitant learn this sensitivity to God's action upon him? Through the rules for discernment, which help him to understand what God is saying to him through his feelings and emotions, through his experience of consolation and desolation.

> I will call it consolation when an interior movement is aroused in the soul, by which it is inflamed with love of its creator and Lord, and as a consequence, can love no creature on the face of the earth for its own sake, but only in the Creator of them all. It is likewise consolation when one sheds tears that move to the love of God .... Finally, I call consolation every increase of faith, hope and love, and all interior joy that invites and attracts to what is heavenly and to the salvation of one's soul by filling it with peace and quiet in its Creator and Lord. (Exx 316)
>
> I call desolation what is entirely the opposite [of consolation], as darkness of soul, turmoil of spirit, inclination to what is low and earthly, restlessness arising from many disturbances and temptations which lead to want of faith, want of hope, want of love. The soul is wholly slothful, tepid, sad and separated, as it were, from its Creator and Lord. (Exx 317)

St Ignatius suggests that one reason for desolation may be that 'God wishes to give us a true knowledge and understanding of ourselves' (Exx 322). These quotations should be sufficient to show the importance St Ignatius gives to the feelings and the emotions, and the respect he shows for the individuality of each person. He was suspect in his day of encouraging illuminism.

What about the over-conceptualisation in the First Principle and Foundation? This is not a part of the *Exercises*, but a preface added after the *Exercises* were written. It is a masterly, but arid, summary of the *Exercises* and may be compared to reading a map before climbing a mountain. Conceptualisation, in the form of maps, is very useful, as every hill-climber knows; but if you do not know what the map signs are really saying, the map can be dangerously misleading. So too, the First Principle and Foundation.

But do not the Exercises instil fear and self-distrust? It is clear from the Annotations that the director must not instil fear and self-distrust. He is to let the exercitant be and let the fear arise from within him, a healthy fear that arises out of a growing awareness of God's goodness. St Ignatius was a man of his time, and thought in the images and within the parameters of sixteenth-century culture. We do not have the same images or the same world-view, and we do not need to try and force ourselves back into the sixteenth century. The grace of God will lead us to know Him in our own images and concepts. We still need to pray for a growing and intense sorrow and tears for our sins, to pray to know ourselves even as we are known.

Because of fear, self-distrust and over-conceptualisation, many who make the Exercises today may be very slow to experience genuine consolation and desolation. They must never be hurried or harassed. Self-knowledge and self-trust can only grow slowly, in an atmosphere of acceptance and gentleness.

In conclusion, the Exercises can be a most effective instrument for the formation of a Christian conscience, provided they are given as St Ignatius advises in the Annotations. If the Annotations are ignored, the Exercises can become a most effective instrument for deforming conscience and destroying faith.

Dying We Live

IN THE FIRST SERMON recorded in Acts, Peter told the crowds: 'You killed him, but God raised him to life' (Acts 2:24). This is the Good News, the essence of Christianity. All the other sermons in Acts are elaborations on the first sermon of Peter.

Some laughed when they heard about the resurrection, others thought that the apostles were drunk; but some believed. On this belief the Church grew and spread.

The message is still being preached. Some laugh when they hear it, others think the preachers are mad; while a growing number of believers have either abandoned belief, or interpret resurrection in such a way that it does not really matter whether Christ rose again or not, whether we live on after death or not. Contemporary society, uncertain what to think about death, prefers *not* to think about it. We are all affected by this attitude. It is extraordinary that while death is the one future event about which we can be absolutely certain, we try to pretend it does not exist; certainly we act as though it did not exist. I have heard patients in some hospitals say that they could always tell when another patient in the ward was dying, because doctors used to hurry past the bed as though no one was in it. In medical schools there are all kinds of courses on the treatment of rare diseases. As far as I know, there are no courses on helping patients to die well. The growing support for euthanasia is, perhaps, symptomatic of our general unwillingness to face death. 'Let's get it over and done with as quickly, as unobtrusively and as expeditiously as possible, and call it—"dying well".' When death does strike, there are elaborate rituals of hiding death. In the United States the patient rarely dies at home; or, if he does, he is laid out after his death in the splendour of a funeral parlour, dressed, painted and padded to look well and comfortable. When the body is eventually committed to the earth, the ground is immediately covered with imitation grass to help the mourners forget the ugly truth. Employees in the funeral business are no longer called 'undertakers'. They have now become 'grief facilitators', which means that they help the mourners not to grieve. Recently I met a social worker who had been told to look after a woman who had attempted suicide several times. The woman's husband had died some months before. She was heartbroken, but all her relatives and friends were telling her 'to snap out of it', and get back to leading a normal life. To be 'normal' means to try and pretend that death does not exist. We do not want to think about it, because we do not know how to think about it. Our vision of life cannot find a place for death except as an ugly ending. We prefer not to think about it. Marshall McLuhan, in *The Mechanical Bride*, writes: 'It is a principle that the failure to face and evaluate unpleasant facts under conditions of art and controlled observation leads to a subsequent avalanche of the disagreeable' — a principle verified in the modern cult of portraying violent death in all its gruesome detail.[1] As Christians we share the contemporary attitude to death; we prefer to concentrate our attention on the social and political dimensions of Jesus' message today, giving little attention to the central message of Christianity.

If modern man does not like facing the thought of death, he is even more disinclined to think about life after death. 'Literally conceived, the idea of an afterlife has no place, makes no sense and is inconsistent within the framework of the contemporary world picture.'[2] We may dislike the statement. We may say, 'if it is true, it is a judgment on contemporary society'. But is it true? If it is true, then we are wasting our time preaching life after death and resurrection to a world which can no longer make any sense of these terms. Some Christian writers, recognising this problem, have

---

[1] Marshall McLuhan, *The Mechanical Bride: Folklore of Industrial Man* (New York: Vanguard, 1951), 15.
[2] Milton Gatch, *Death: Meaning and Mortality in Christian Thought and Contemporary Culture* (New York: Seabury, 1969), 184.

avoided it by interpreting resurrection so that it does not upset 'the contemporary world picture'. Milton Gatch, for example, says:

> The issue raised by the conflict between immortality [by which he means life after death of the soul without the body] and resurrection [of the body] has never been more crucial than at present, even although we must speak of immortality and resurrection not as facts, but as modes of approach to life.[3]

Immortality, then, comes to mean the individualist approach to life, resurrection means community existence, and death means annihilation. Another, Dr Schubert Ogden, writes: 'But what I must refuse to accept, precisely as a Christian theologian, is that belief in our subjective existence after death is in some way a necessary article of Christian belief'.[4] And a third, Paul van Buren, explains the resurrection as a figurative way of expressing the influence of Christ's life and work and words on the apostles.[5] Another states even more categorically: 'Jesus' work of bringing certainty to men was completed when he died abandoned by God and men'.[6]

In view of these contemporary attitudes to death and interpretations of the resurrection, how are we to stand as Catholics? When I was a university chaplain, I used to hear students say, 'I don't think I'm a Catholic any more. I can no longer believe in ...' it might be God's existence, or transubstantiation, or infallibility, or life after death. I then used to ask them why they could not believe, and in listening I was treated to some extraordinary private theology. On life after death, for example, I would hear a grotesque theology in which vaguely remembered ancient myths, horrifying paintings of the Last Judgment, bits of Dante's *Inferno*, ghost stories, hellfire

---
[3] Gatch, *Death*, 185.
[4] Schubert Ogden, *Reality of God and Other Essays* (London: SCM, 1967), 230.
[5] Paul van Buren, *The Secular Meaning of the Gospel* (Harmondsworth: Penguin, 1963).
[6] Gerhard Ebeling, *Theology and Proclamation* (London: Collins, 1966), 91.

sermons and the New Testament accounts were all mixed up together. It was good that they did not believe their own picture: sad that they should therefore abandon all belief in life after death.

This article is not an attempt to give a clear explanation of what we mean by life after death and resurrection. There is no clear explanation this side of the grave. It is possible only to offer some reflections on our attitude to doctrine in general, and to the doctrine of life after death and of the resurrection in particular. I hope these reflections may help to remove some of the fears which prevent us seeing our lives in the perspective of death and resurrection, and so rob us of the Good News.

In his first introductory observation to the *Spiritual Exercises*, St Ignatius describes their purpose:

> We call Spiritual Exercises every way of preparing and disposing the soul to rid itself of all inordinate attachments and, after their removal, of seeking and finding the will of God in the disposition of our life for the salvation of our souls. (Exx 1)

Disordered attachments are usually thought of in the context of pleasure and comfort, status and wealth, honour and pride. But much more subtle, and more difficult to eradicate, are our inordinate attachments to our preconceived ideas about God, the Church and ourselves. We may hardly be aware of them because they are so much part of ourselves; but they can prevent us from opening our minds and hearts to God. Without being fully conscious that we are doing so, we prefer to keep God at a safe distance. Our preconceived ideas of doctrine in general, and of the doctrine of life after death and resurrection in particular, may constitute such an 'inordinate attachment' and stifle our growth.

Doctrine does not flutter down from heaven ready published in neat sentences. The doctrinal statements of the Church are conceptual expressions of the faith experience of the Church, expressed in the language and thought-categories of their time. They are given to us for our guidance, to help us discern our own experience of God's action in our lives. If we are not trying to live a life of faith, if we are not trying to respond with our lives to the truth that God loves us, then doctrinal statements cannot help us. Doctrine is not the primary object of faith. The God of mystery, the wholly Other, who revealed Himself in Christ, is the primary object of faith. Doctrines are a means, given to us by the Church, to help us understand who He is and who we are; but they are only a means. To consider them as the primary object of faith would be idolatry. Doctrines may be compared to maps, indispensable to the pilgrim in his journey through life, but no use to him if he does not get off his seat and start moving. If in his life he is either sitting still or moving away from God—attacking his neighbour viciously, for example—he is off the map. Maps are useless to us unless we can locate ourselves on them. That is why 'orthopraxis', that is, trying to find God by being honest, searching for truth and sharing our lives, is the basic constituent of 'orthodoxy'; and why it is so ridiculous when people attack each other viciously in the name of orthodoxy. This is also why the attitude to doctrine in general among so many 'loyal' Catholics, which leads them to accept it unquestioningly and unreflectively, is, in fact, unorthodoxy. If we act in this way we are like lost travellers, afraid to take out the map in case we lose faith in it—a sure sign that we *have* lost faith in it. To be helped by the map, we have to be on the road, and we need to take our bearings: that is, if the Church's teaching is to be of any help to us, we must be trying to live a life of faith; we must consult our own experience, be in touch with ourselves and reflect on our lives. The importance of this in our attitude to the doctrine of life after death will be discussed later.

Doctrine, too, is presented to us by the Church not as a final answer to our questions. The phrase *Roma locuta est, causa finita est* has been lifted out of its context and applied to doctrine generally, with disastrous consequences. A doctrine of the Church does not claim to give the complete answer. To continue the map analogy, the function of doctrine is to keep us from falling over cliffs and getting lost down cul-de-sacs. It does not claim to give us a complete description of the route. The doctrine of life after death and resurrection, for example, tells us hardly anything about either; but it does prevent us wandering down the cul-de-sac 'death equals annihilation'. Therefore we should look on doctrine not as a threat, the unintelligible *obiter dicta* of a grim headmaster, to be recited daily under threat of expulsion. Rather, doctrine is God's gift to us through the Church. He wants to reveal His love for us and teach us, in the light of it, to love as we are loved. The Church's understanding of who God is, and of her own nature, is a developing understanding. Our individual understanding of who God is, of the meaning of the Church, of our own lives, is equally a developing understanding. In all our learning we learn, or should learn, as much by our mistakes as by our successes. We have to stumble if we are to learn to walk. Doctrine is often presented in such a threatening way that it paralyzes us. We are afraid to try walking in case we stumble and become heretics. So we prefer to sit still, which is the greatest heresy of all. The heretic has at least started moving. The trouble is that he insists that stumbling down a cul-de-sac is the only way to move.

In sum, we should look on doctrine as the gift of a loving God. As the expression of the faith of the Church, it will be intelligible to us only in so far as we are trying to live a life of faith. Our understanding grows and develops. Formulations which helped us to find God, or at least did not cause difficulty, at one period of our lives, may become obstacles at a later stage. Many of us in the Church today find that belief in life after death and resurrection, accepted at one stage without difficulty, has now become a doctrine which we prefer not to think about in case we find ourselves denying it.

In the final part of this article I shall give a very brief sketch of some of my own stumblings in trying to understand life after death and resurrection, and of some reflections which I have found helpful. I only hope that they do not lead readers down a cul-de-sac.

For a long time I believed in the resurrection as in the other mysteries of the faith because I was brought up a Catholic and saw no reason to deny them. The resurrection, I was taught, was the best attested event in ancient history and it proved Christ's divinity beyond any shadow of doubt. We, too, will rise again with the same bodies at the day of judgment, when, we go for all eternity either to heaven or hell. The period between death and resurrection will be spent either in hell, or part- or full-time in purgatory or, if we have been exceptionally good and/or gained the requisite indulgences, in heaven. Then the doubts began to cloud this clear picture. I was unable to imagine what resurrection could possibly feel like; there were problems about cannibals' victims, doubts about the existence of this invisible, intangible, imperceptible and, to me, unintelligible entity called the soul, thoughts about the unfairness of indulgences and the gross injustice of hell. Heaven, too, became increasingly unattractive. Saints' lives left the impression of a place populated by austere men and women, and some dreadful children, whose virtue seemed to lie in the severity of their penances. It was all so far removed from a world where a world war was being fought. These doubts and misgivings were at one level of consciousness, but there was another level which refused to pay them any attention and knew that God was good. When I became a Jesuit and made the thirty-day retreat, I could pray on the events of Christ's life and on his passion, but the resurrection was a disappointment. I prayed St Ignatius' petition, 'To ask for the grace to be glad and rejoice intensely because of the great joy and glory of Christ Our Lord', but it never came. The resurrection was an event outside of me and the joy was a forced joy, not to be compared to the joy of seeing my family again or the indefinable longing and hope I could experience by watching the sunset and reflecting that God is in all things and all things are in Him.

When I began to learn a little more about scripture, the doubts increased. I learnt that belief in life after death and resurrection of the body was a late development in Judaism. The great patriarchs and prophets had got along without belief in heaven. Then there were the exegetes demythologizing the New Testament. It was like watching the tide come in and demolish my sandcastles. The resurrection sandcastle was untouched for some time, until I began to look more closely at the New Testament accounts of Christ's appearances after his death and saw how conflicting they really were. The usual explanation of the discrepancies was that the resurrection was such a staggering event that the apostles' confusion was only to be expected. I found this explanation nonsense. The more extraordinary an event, the more likely we are to remember it in vivid detail. The resurrection accounts are not even sure where the appearances took place, whether in Jerusalem or Galilee. According to John, the body was anointed immediately after Christ's death, according to Luke and Mark, it was to be anointed later, in Matthew there was no anointing because the tomb was already sealed. In Mark three women visit the tomb, in Matthew, two. In Mark and John the tomb is already open, in Matthew an angel moves the stone as the women approach. In Mark there is a young man in dazzling white, in Luke there are two men and in John the angel is displaced by Christ himself. Luke denies that any women had seen Jesus at the tomb and so contradicts Matthew and John. In Matthew, Christ is already ascended when he appears to the apostles and tells them he will be with them until the end of time. In John the risen Christ confers the Spirit. In Luke the ascension takes place forty days after the resurrection and the Holy Spirit is given later. All the witnesses to the resurrection are believers. Not all of them recognise him immediately. It takes two of them a walk and a meal before they recognise with whom they are talking. Paul, in 1 Corinthians 15, includes his own Damascus vision with the appearances to the apostles, as though in the same category. The tide was well in now, and lapping away at the resurrection sandcastle.

The answer given to all these difficulties was that the Gospels are not to be understood simply as factual accounts of Christ's life and words. The Gospels are also theological reflections of the early Church on the meaning of Christ, not straight biography.

I could see the truth in this answer and accept it; and it cleared up many difficulties. But it still left the question: when I say, 'I believe in the resurrection of the Body and life everlasting', what am I believing in? What actually happened at Christ's resurrection?

The New Testament accounts make it quite clear that they are not describing the resuscitation of a corpse. John and Luke, for example, emphasize that the disciples did not recognise Christ straight away. Also Christ comes and goes in the appearances, passing through closed doors in a very non-bodily way. Paul's vision does not mention the body. There are no witnesses of the resurrection event itself, but only of Christ risen. The faith of the Church is not in the empty tomb, a historical fact, in principle verifiable. The faith of the Church is that Christ has overcome death, is risen, is Lord of the Universe. That Christ died is a historical fact. That he rose again and is Lord of all history is not in the same category of events.

The New Testament expresses the faith of the early Church. The resurrection accounts express and reflect on the apostles' experience of Christ after his death. The apostles proclaimed that unique and mysterious experience in the thought-categories of their world, in the ideas and images which could best approximate to their experience. No human formulation can ever be adequate to describe the God of mystery, either in Himself or in His actions. The apostles experienced Christ in a mysterious way after his death. They expressed that experience in the words, 'God has raised this man Jesus to life. Jesus is both Lord and Christ': this was the content of their message.[7] It was for them the most real event in their lives.

---

[7] See Acts 2: 36.

Something had happened to them which was not merely subjective. Attempts made to explain away the resurrection in psychological terms, or to reduce it to some inner-worldly event, cannot explain the New Testament accounts and the subsequent history of Christianity. The apostles' experience of the risen Christ transformed them from being frightened, disillusioned men into fearless men who proclaimed the resurrection, a message which was to lead most of them to martyrdom. Some who heard them laughed, others thought they were drunk, some believed. Within the hearts of the believers, the apostles' preaching found a resonance. They could accept that Christ was risen again, and in accepting this truth their own lives were changed, and they came closer to God and to their fellow men. For the believers, the apostles' message was not just a piece of information to be learnt and repeated on religious occasions. It was a message which brought them new life there and then, transformed their attitudes to wealth, honour, status and, above all, to each other, and it gave a new sense of urgency to their lives. They were now on a journey, not to extinction, annihilation, or to flit among the shadows of Sheol, but to meet and be dissolved into the risen Christ.

The same message is preached to us. Does it bring new life and transform us?

If Christ is risen, then it is a truth not simply of the past, with future reference beyond the grave; but it is one which must affect us now. 'Be still and know that I am God!' (Psalm 46:10): 'Be still and know that I am risen again, that I am with you now, that I am the Lord who has conquered death.' We must be still before this message. We must empty our minds, for the moment, of all our theology, our imaginings, our misconceptions. Listening trustingly, without worrying about ourselves, our faith or lack of it, is all-mportant. For it is in stillness that he can open our eyes, and we can begin to recognise him in the breaking of bread.

'Jesus is Lord.' He has sunk into the depths of our sinfulness, hopelessness and despair, and he is risen again. There is no depth in our life, no situation, no crisis where he is not present. Perhaps, for some of us, it is only in crises that we begin to see what resurrection means.

If we go to meet him, we shall find him. I find those theologians very helpful who emphasize the resurrection as an event which is happening to us now. They have seized on a truth which we have tended to ignore:

> I take the risk of doing what he [Jesus] asks, contrary to all human reason. In the course of so doing I experience the fact: it is true …. Suddenly, you take the risk again, contrary to all reason, and then again, and yet again. And one day you discover that you are on the path through *this* life *to* life.[8]

Belief in the resurrection is not simply belief in a past event for Christ, and a future event for us. It is a belief, too, about our life at present, that the risen Christ is with us. The truth of the mystery dawns on us in so far as we try to live selflessly, and have times when we try to be still and know that he is with us.

But what about life after death? Are we to interpret resurrection as a way of talking about this present life, face the fact that death means annihilation? The theologians who emphasize the resurrection as a present event have helped to confirm my faith in life after death and resurrection. In trying to be still and let the truth of his resurrection break in, it seems to be truth too good and too great to be fleeting, to end in death and be no more. 'The mountains may crumble and the hills depart, but my love for you remains forever.' (Isaiah 54:10) Why forever, if we only last for a few years between nothingness and extinction? I cannot imagine life after death or resurrection and do not try to. 'Seek first the kingdom of God' presumably applies to thought about life after death as well as tomorrow's dinner. Paul says, 'We shall be changed. Our present

---

[8] Willi Marxsen, *The Resurrection of Jesus of Nazareth* (Philadelphia: Fortress, 1970), 184.

perishable nature must put on imperishability and this mortal nature must put on immortality.' (1 Corinthians 15:53) It is as though in our lives we are like drops of water suspended above the ocean, separate, isolated, wanting to be one with it. At death we are dissolved into a new kind of existence, into an at-one-ness with God, from whom we came. Yet if there is not some measure of individuality, some identity with our existence now, life after death, described as at-one-ness, becomes annihilation. The New Testament accounts emphasize the identity between Jesus on earth and the risen Jesus. What we do on earth, how we have lived, the friends we have had, our at-one-ness with others and with creation, must bear some relation to our life after death. If heaven is pie in the sky, we are mixing in some of the ingredients now. These thoughts give urgency to life. Von Hügel summed it up well when he said that Christians must aim at otherworldliness without fanaticism and this-worldliness without philistinism.[9]

Finally, another thought which I have found helpful: 'Individuals die within a matter of a few years, and we have no reason to suppose that their life continues beyond the grave'.[10] But what is life this side of the grave? What are these bodies in which we live? We experience them as flesh and blood, but what are they? 'Largely empty space', the scientists tell us: a conglomeration of energy charges. We grow from babyhood through adolescence to the grave. We eat the same food, drink the same drink, breathe the same air, and yet remain our separate, incommunicable selves. I wonder if there are creatures on some other planet who are totally different from ourselves, and who have heard rumours of man. Perhaps their theologians have had seminars on us and produced a consensus

---

[9] Friedrich von Hügel, *Eternal Life: A Study of Its Implications and Applications* (Edinburgh: T. and T. Clark, 1913), 255.
[10] Gordon D. Kaufman, *Systematic Theology: A Historicist Perspective* (New York: Charles Scribner's Sons, 1968), 464.

paper: 'Literally conceived, the idea of man has no place, makes no sense and is inconsistent within the framework of our contemporary world picture'. As one writer puts it: 'Christian apologetics would do better to draw attention to the absurdity of suggesting that our bodies are material now, than to try to defend the position that they will be material then'.[11] Resurrection becomes less improbable the more we reflect on the improbability of our present existence.

Our belief in resurrection does not take away our fear of death or desire to live. It makes this life all the more important and precious. Christ was afraid of death. We do not have to be braver. But it is fear in hope, fear of birth into a new life. And our life is a rehearsal for this new birth through death. We have a solemn rehearsal at every Mass when we give ourselves to the Father in Christ. 'Take and eat, this is my Body, given for you. Do this in commemoration of me.' If we try to do the same in memory of him and see our lives as a gift to be given so that others may live, then he gives us some glimmer of his goodness and leads us on to hope for our final birth into a life where the bonds which enclose us now in space and time are broken, and we shall be at one with him in whom all creation has its being.

---

[11] M. E. Dahl, *Resurrection of the Body* (London: SCM, 1962), 91.

Forgotten Truths of the Spiritual Exercises

'AND THEN I HAVE TO fit in a retreat sometime.' So ends the sentence of many a priest and religious as they try to work out their programme for the summer. For Jesuits, an annual eight-day retreat has been part of the rule since 1608, over fifty years after St Ignatius' death; and many other religious orders have adopted the same rule. Official documents of popes and Jesuit generals recommend the Exercises of St Ignatius with enthusiastic praise for their wonderful effects. Those who have to make them do not always share that same enthusiasm, but keep their grumbles to themselves or to a select group of friends. This article takes a selection of these grumbles as a means of rediscovering truths about the Exercises which many of us had forgotten.

In 1957, the extensive *Bibliographie ignatienne, 1894–1957* was published.[1] Another bibliography is being prepared, with over 2,000 titles, for the period 1957–75.[2] The weight of all this scholarship can crush the amateur retreat director. He has not the time to read the current literature, but is vaguely aware that his own understanding and method of giving the Exercises are now considered out of date. Reactions vary. Some, suspicious of all that is new, continue as before, only more so, describing 'the length and breadth of hell' in even more vivid detail, and bemoaning the declining numbers of retreatants. Others, who have always been a little uncertain about their own ability to understand and give the Exercises but have continued trying, have become even more diffident. I count myself among those who grumble at having to make the Exercises and

---

[1] *Bibliographie ignatienne, 1894–1957: classement méthodique des livres et articles concernant saint Ignace de Loyola, sa vie, les Exercices spirituels, les Constitutions, ses autres écrits et sa spiritualité*, edited by Jean-François Gilmont and Paul Daman (Paris: Desclée de Brouwer, 1957).
[2] Paul Begheyn, 'A Bibliography on St Ignatius' *Spiritual Exercises*: A Working Tool for American Students', *Studies in the Spirituality of Jesuits*, 8/2 (March, 1981).

among the diffident who give them. Recently, I have had some time to read ancient and modern commentaries on the Exercises, and to meet people who are specialists in Ignatian spirituality. It has been an encouraging experience, which I should like to pass on to those who do not have the time.³

Grumbles

1. 'If I hear once again that man is created to praise, reverence and serve God, I'll scream': a sister's reaction after yet another Jesuit retreat. Men react less dramatically: 'I reread old copies of the school magazine', said one Jesuit whom I knew. For him it was certainly true that 'it is not much knowledge that fills and satisfies the soul, but the intimate understanding and relish' of all that had ever happened at the school of his youth, where he always made his annual retreat. We may never have been driven to screaming or reading the old school magazine, but we know the boredom which repetition can induce.

2. Another reflection on the Exercises from the old-school-magazine friend: 'I never have understood all this consolation–desolation business; I suppose it is something which afflicts hot-blooded foreigners. I usually feel much-of-a-muchness myself, occasionally dropping into a mild depression at retreat times.'

3. As retreat director I met a very unhappy and broken religious who, on being asked, 'Have you not spoken to anyone about this before?', answered, 'Yes, many times, but I am always told to practise the third mode of humility'. This is one example among many of the damage that the Exercises can do. Far from liberating, they can often be given and made in such a way that they cripple the retreatant, imprison the spirit and engender religious nausea rather than the love of God.

---

³ There is an excellent series of articles on the Exercises and Ignatian spirituality, produced by the Program to Adapt the Spiritual Exercises. Articles from this series are referred to as PASE.

4. The experience of many in making the Exercises may be compared to riding a bicycle which has no chain. One may pedal away vigorously at the meditations and additions, but somehow the Exercises do not engage with real life. One retreat giver, after exhorting his retreatants to 'go in spirit with St Francis Xavier and lick those lepers' wounds', was later heard by one of them complaining loudly at breakfast about the quality of the marmalade. We can all identify with that retreat giver.

5. Eulogies of the Exercises by popes, bishops, Jesuit generals and retreat givers can sometimes give the impression that they are a kind of magic. 'Are you worried, anxious, bewildered, confused, lukewarm? Try the Exercises and become a fully integrated, dynamic Christian, apostolic witness and eschatological sign.' The Exercises are enjoying a vogue at present, especially among religious. 'Solve your problems with a thirty-day retreat.' If the Exercises are treated as a magic panacea for the ills of our day, we shall reap a rich harvest of problems.

6. This last remark leads on to a final grumble. Recent writings, emphasizing the damage the Exercises can do, the skill required in a director, etc., can lead the amateur to despair of ever being able to make or give them.

* * *

I think these are useful grumbles, because they can remind us of forgotten truths.

1. In the time of St Ignatius, and for many years after his death, the Exercises were normally given to individuals, not to groups. In 1584, Fr Crusius, a master of novices in Germany, wrote to the Jesuit General, Fr Acquaviva, asking if he might give the Exercises to groups of three to six novices. He had obviously been trying this already, because he tells Acquaviva of the great advantages in group retreats: the novices encourage each other, are more ready

to discuss their meditations in a group, and make the meditations better because they know they will have to discuss them afterwards! Acquaviva's reply is interesting. He writes that group retreats are contrary to the tradition of giving the Exercises, because different people have different needs and their individual needs cannot be answered in a group. In public discussions, the novices will talk generalities and not about their own experience. If there are not enough directors to give individually guided retreats, then Fr Crusius should do what they do in Rome, namely cut down the length of each individual retreat.[4]

'Different people have different needs.' Therefore there is no one form of the Exercises suitable for all. They must be adapted to the needs of each individual retreatant. The reason why we feel bored with retreats is because, in the form in which we make them or are given them, they no longer answer our needs. St Ignatius himself does not seem to have envisaged the Exercises being repeated annually for eight days. Nadal, his trusted interpreter, saw the purpose of the thirty-day retreat in the noviceship as an initiation into Jesuit spirituality, which would then become a way of life. Once the Exercises begin to 'take', the retreatant may well want to spend some time in prayer and quiet; but there should be a growing freedom in prayer and the manner of it. There is a false glorification of the Exercises which treats them as though they were magic. 'Keep on making them, and they will work, provided you have the right dispositions.' When they do not appear to work, the answer must be that we do not have the right dispositions; so we try again, until repeated dissatisfaction ensures that we never shall have the right dispositions. Boredom with the Exercises may well be a very healthy sign that we should no longer be making them in the form in which we are accustomed. We should pay more attention to our boredom.

---

[4] G. A. Hugh, *The Exercises for Individuals and Groups* (Jersey City: PASE, 1960); also in *Woodstock Letters*, 89 (April 1960), 127–172.

2. In his preliminary observations to the book of the *Exercises*, St Ignatius writes (Annotation 6):

> When the one who is giving the Exercises perceives that the exercitant is not affected by any spiritual experiences, such as consolations or desolations, and that he is not troubled by different spirits, he ought to ply him with questions about the Exercises. He should ask him whether he makes them at the appointed times and how he makes them.

Ignatius expects the retreatant, even Englishmen, to have these experiences. Unless they have them, the retreat cannot continue, because it is through consolation and desolation that we come to discern what God's will is in our lives. The central importance of this experience is another commonly forgotten truth. Pelagianism, always a temptation for Anglo-Saxons, can creep into the Exercises, turning them into an endurance test: will-strengthening exercises designed to produce valiant men and women ready to advance under withering fire, heedless of life and limb and, consequently, of their own feelings. Desolation comes to be regarded as something to be snapped out of; and consolation is a feeling to he treated with circumspection, if not suspicion. Relying on the word of Ignatius, that 'love ought to manifest itself in deeds rather than in words', and adding 'or in feelings', we feel justified in paying scant attention to the consolation–desolation talk. Yet this was not the mind of St Ignatius, for whom feelings were of primary importance. The Exercises are designed to help us discover the will of God in our lives, not by ignoring our feelings but by listening to them, coming to know them and learning how to interpret them. The power of the Exercises, the need for skilled direction, lies precisely in this point. The Exercises, the Society of Jesus, began, in a sense, with Ignatius' own feelings, when he was lying wounded at Loyola. He read romances, he dreamed of courtly love and daring deeds. He also read the lives of the saints and Ludolph's *Life of Christ*. He noticed that his day-dreams left him in a sad mood; whilst his thoughts on Christ and on the lives of the saints continued to attract him. These were not feelings he aroused in himself. They just happened. But he did not just snap out of them. He reflected on them, and this was the start of his discernment of spirits. He was uneducated in letters, in theology, in spirituality. He observed his moods in relation to his conscious activity, he came to know them, to be less naïve and more circumspect in discerning them, but he never stopped listening to them. It became a lifelong and continuous habit. Every decision, even the apparently most minute, was tested in this way. He tested his decisions, not against some external criterion, a practice which would have driven him insane, but on the criterion of the at-one-ness of his whole being which he had given over to Christ. He entrusted himself to Christ, an instrument in his hands, and therefore believed that if in some decision he was going against God's will, the disharmony would sooner or later manifest itself in his feelings of consolation and desolation.

Favre, while giving a retreat to Peter Canisius in 1543, wrote:

> I observe more clearly than ever certain evident signs for proceeding in the Exercises: how important it is for the discernment of spirits to see if we are attentive to ideas and reflections or rather to the Spirit itself, which appears through desires, motions, ardour or despondency, tranquillity or anxiety, joy or sorrow, and other analogous spiritual motions. For it is in these motions much more easily than in thoughts that one can pass judgment on the soul and its quests.[5]

Thus, the matter for discernment is the involuntary feelings and moods which arise in and from the meditations. This is the subject matter for discussion with the director. Through trying to articulate

---

[5] Pierre Favre, *Memoriale*, in *Beati Petri Fabri. Epistolae, Memoriale et Processus*, MHSJ 48 (Madrid: Institutum Historicum Societatis Iesu, 1914), 638–639; English in *The Spiritual Writings of Pierre Favre*, translated by Edmond C. Murphy and Martin E. Palmer (St Louis: Institute of Jesuits Sources, 1996), 240; and cf. P. Robb, *The Retreatant in a Directed Retreat* (Jersey City: PASE, 1972).

these feelings and moods, we become more aware of them. In one of his directories of the Exercises, St Ignatius says that exercitants may be encouraged to write down their reflections and feelings (*conceptus et motiones*).[6] The function of the director is to help the retreatant to get in touch with his feelings and learn to discern them, not to discern them for him. If the retreatant does not learn to discern for himself, the Exercises will have no lasting effect.

Herein lie both the difficulty and the importance of the Exercises today. In Western countries we have fostered the intellect and despised the emotions, thus becoming more cerebral than sensitive. We have developed a wonderful technology which threatens to extinguish human life either sooner, by nuclear war, or later, by pollution of the environment and exhaustion of vital resources. If we lose touch with our feelings, we become inhuman and capable of a terrifying callousness to the sufferings of others. Hence the phenomenon of ardent supporters of social justice imprisoning, torturing and killing those who oppose their particular theory. We keep on hearing about the misery and needs of the Third World; but the information stays in our heads and the Third World grows poorer. In the promotion of social justice we need information, but unless the information touches our hearts as well as our heads, it will have no effect. That is why the Exercises have such a valuable contribution to make in the Church's mission of justice and peace.

The experience of consolation–desolation is not easy for us today, because the pace of life and our very conceptual education can so easily keep us out of touch with ourselves. Even in the sixteenth century, when the pace of life was so much slower, Pierre Favre writes of pious retreatants who do not seem to experience any consolation–desolation:

---

[6] *Directoria Exercitiorum Spiritualium (1540–1599)*, MHSJ 76 (Rome: Institutum Historicum Societatis Iesu, 1955), 3. 2. English in *On Giving the Spiritual Exercises: The Early Manuscript Directories and the Official Directory of 1599*, translated and edited by Martin E. Palmer (St Louis: Institute of Jesuit Sources, 1996).

However, holy as they may be, lead them on to examine themselves in terms of a higher degree of perfection in their lives and conduct; then you will see two spirits appear, one a source of strength, the other of darkness, one of justice, the other of degradation.[7]

To become aware of our feelings, we need to articulate them in writing and in talking with a director. But we can only do this with a director who can treat us gently and not judge us. 'If the director observes that the exercitant is in desolation and tempted, let him not deal severely and harshly, but gently and kindly.' (Annotation 7) Because of the difficulty of experiencing consolation–desolation, an individual may require a long preparatory period before beginning the Exercises. Favre, for example, before he began the Exercises with Dr Cochlaeus, spent several hours daily for several weeks in conversation with him. Ignatius was four years with Favre himself before giving him the Exercises. There are other reasons, too, why retreatants may require a long preliminary period before beginning the Exercises: for example, their basic notion of God may be so tinged with unacknowledged fear, or resentment, or scrupulosity that to plunge them into the Exercises may only accentuate their difficulties.

So far, the answers I have given are open to the charge that the Exercises encourage and foster a spiritual narcissism. There is one prayer in the Exercises, the only one which never varies in all the meditations: 'I will beg God our Lord for the grace that all my intentions, actions and operations may be directed purely to the service and praise of His Divine Majesty.' The Exercises are not centred on our feelings and emotions; they are centred on Christ. It is in the light of God's revelation in Christ, and in the faith that 'God is in all things and all things in Him' that we consider ourselves.

---

[7] Favre, *Memoriale*, 639 (*Spiritual Writings of Pierre Favre*, 241); cf. Robb, *Retreatant in a Directed Retreat*.

'What have I done for him? What will I do for him?' The Exercises are designed to lead us gradually into this light. Too much light blinds, which is another way of expressing grumble no. 3 on the danger of the Exercises.

3. St Ignatius' own teaching on this point is given clearly in the Annotations:

> Let him [the director] adhere to the points and add only a short summary explanation. The reason for this is that when one in meditating takes the solid foundation of the facts and goes over it and reflects on it for himself, he may find something that makes them a little clearer or better understood. For it is not much knowledge that satisfies and fills the soul but the intimate understanding and relish of the truth (Annotation 2).

'It may happen that in the first week some are slower in attaining what is sought.' (Annotation 4) No one is to be hurried. Most of the retreats given by the early Jesuits did not go beyond the First Week; and this included retreats to bishops, abbots and vicars-general. In Annotation 11, Ignatius writes:

> While the exercitant is engaged in the first week of the Exercises, it will be helpful if he knows nothing of what is to be done in the second week. Rather, let him labour to attain what he is seeking in the first week, as if he hoped to find no good in the second.

The exercitant has to learn to go at his own pace. To be coerced or hurried on by an enthusiastic director can damage the exercitant. I am still grateful for two points in particular which we were given in an excellent preached retreat some twenty years ago. One was that we should look on prayer time not as a duty, but as a gift: if you want to use the time in prayer, do so; but there is no compulsion. Somehow, when the pressure of 'duty' was removed, the desire to pray could grow. The other point was the director's preliminary observation on the third mode of humility. He said he was reluctant to talk about it in case he was waving us up a mountain which he had not climbed himself. His honesty was encouraging and helped us to see the third mode of humility as an invitation, not a command.

To conclude this answer to grumble no. 3, and a fuller answer to grumble no. 1: the exercitant must be allowed to go at his or her own pace. That is why there must be a great variety of ways in which one makes the annual retreat. Some people may be over-worked, over-tired, over-anxious. They may need a few days of quiet idleness without even attempting to pray. Others may feel that they are growing increasingly isolated, anti-social, dogmatic. They may need some form of community retreat. Others, whose work leaves them little time for reading, may need a 'preached retreat' which includes informative conferences. Others again may need solitude and withdrawal with plenty of time for prayer on their own, perhaps on only one part of one meditation of the Exercises. The director must never force the pace. We do damage not so much by our own ignorance, or failure to live up to the ideals we profess, as by refusing to acknowledge our own ignorance and failures.

4. The fourth grumble was about the unreality of retreats: lepers' wounds and marmalade. The Exercises are designed to help the exercitant become a contemplative in action. This cannot happen in eight days, or even in thirty. In a retreat we can withdraw for eight or thirty days to learn a method of prayer which can open us up to God and help us to begin to experience Him in a new way in our lives; but this is only a beginning. The Contemplation for obtaining Love, for example, is not an annual event to be fitted in with the packing on the eighth day. It is to become a permanent attitude, 'to find God in all things, and all things in Him'. Ignatius the mystic was also Ignatius the practical administrator. He could weep at the sight of a flower and then give his whole attention to very mundane details of daily living. The Spanish Jesuits of his time were all for more prayer. Fr Oviedo, the rector of Gandia, was a three-hour-daily-prayer man. Nadal, on his return from Spain, told

Ignatius that he had agreed to the Spaniards' request for one-and-a-half hours' prayer daily. Nadal describes Ignatius' reaction. 'He sharply denounced me in the presence of others and thereafter made no great use of my services.' Da Câmara, in the *Memoriale*, reports that Ignatius said it was

> ... his opinion, from which no one would ever move him, that, for those who are studying, one hour of prayer was sufficient (two examens of conscience plus the divine office), it being supposed that they are practising mortification and self-denial.[8]

To use a later analogy, the Exercises are not a battery-charging operation, but a way of learning how to be self-charging in our ordinary occupations. It is a continuous process, which we only assimilate slowly and gradually. Those who do learn it, as Ignatius did, are capable of turning to prayer from the most exacting occupations. The work helps their prayer, and the prayer helps their work. This leads us back to an earlier point: the need for honesty in the Exercises, bringing our whole person into them, warts and all. Otherwise we cannot find God in all things, but only in that ideal image of ourselves which we bring out at retreat time and put away again on the eighth day. There is less danger of unreality in what are termed 'Nineteenth Annotation retreats':

> One who is educated or talented, but engaged in public affairs or necessary business, should take one and a half hours daily for the Spiritual Exercises (Annotation 19).

5. The answers given to the first four grumbles contain the answer to grumble no. 5, on the danger of considering the Exercises to be

---

[8] *Fontes narrativi de S. Ignatio de Loyola*, volume 1, MHSJ 66 (Rome: Institutum Historicum Societatis Iesu, 1943), 676–677; English in *Remembering Iñigo: Glimpses of the Life of St Ignatius of Loyola: The Memoriale of Luís Gonçalves da Câmara*, translated by Alexander Eaglestone and Joseph A. Munitiz (Leominster: Gracewing, 2004), n. 255. See Robert E. McNally, *Prayer and the Early Society of Jesus* (Jersey City: PASE, 1965); also printed in *Woodstock Letters*, 94 (Spring 1965), 190–234.

a magic remedy for our ills. If the exercitant is not ready to begin them, if they are not adapted to his needs, if there is not a careful discernment of consolation–desolation, and if the Exercises are not 'earthed' into the actual life experience of the exercitant, then they will not produce their effects. The Exercises are designed to help us to grow in the knowledge and love of God according to our talents, energies and abilities, and the grace he gives us. Any attempts to reach sanctity by a short cut, which ignores us as we really are, is like trying to jump a mountain: a useless expenditure of energy which can land us flat on our faces.

6. I hope the effect of these reflections has not been the opposite of what I intended, discouraging instead of encouraging the diffident amateur to make or give the Exercises. Ignatius says:

> We call Spiritual Exercises every way of preparing and disposing the soul to rid itself of all inordinate attachments, and, after their removal, of seeking and finding the will of God in the disposition of our life for the salvation of our soul (Annotation 1).

There are hundreds of ways of 'preparing'. That is why it is to indulge in pedantry to worry and argue about what is to be termed Spiritual Exercises and what is not. Are school retreats of one to three days, with a few talks each day, to be called Spiritual Exercises? What about Sunday afternoon retreats? All these activities can 'prepare and dispose the soul'. But some people will feel the need for something more, and may want to make an eight-day or thirty-day retreat. To direct someone in such a retreat does require skill and training. The greater the skill, the more we can help. Many of us know we are not skilled, but would like to be. If we try to be honest with ourselves and do not try to coerce the exercitant, then though we may not give them all the help they need, at least our willingness to be with them will be of some help, and we shall not damage them. Practice will make us more honest and less likely to force or coerce. In St Ignatius' own time, novices were giving the Exercises. Once Laínez, in Parma, was invited to give lectures in a convent of eighty nuns. The tailor to the convent had been given the Exercises by a Jesuit novice. He suggested to one of the nuns that she should try the same. The nun asked Laínez to give her the Exercises. Then a few more came, till eventually the whole convent was asking. Laínez began to direct some of them and then handed them over to a Jesuit novice to complete the retreats.[9] If in Ignatius' time there had been a well-educated and talented body of laity, he would have had them giving the Exercises. After all, he was a layman himself when he began giving them. It is good to know that the practice is being reintroduced.

Finally, to whom should the Exercises be given? According to Nadal, the Exercises can be given to every class of people, including heretics and pagans. (Some would claim that we have been doing this for years in our school retreats!) The Exercises may be given to pagans, according to Nadal, provided they can be brought to believe in one God and pray to Him. Such exercises will include the Principle and Foundation, the meditations of the First Week (excluding confession and communion); whilst the Kingdom and the Two Standards can be given and referred to the one God. If all these exercises are completed, an election, adapted to the individual, is in order. With 'heretics', Nadal says that the director should prescind from those truths which are unacceptable to the heretic. During the Second Week meditations, simple contemplations and application of the senses are to be preferred to subtle intellectual speculations.[10]

In Ignatius's own lifetime, a time of rapid change, when old structures were falling and everything was being questioned, the

---

[9] See Hugh, *Exercises for Individuals and Groups*.
[10] Joseph F. X. Erhart, 'Doctrine of Father Jerome Nadal on the Spiritual Exercises of St Ignatius', in *The 1967 Workshop on the Spiritual Exercises* (Jersey City: PASE, 1967); also in *Woodstock Letters*, 82 (November 1953), 317–334.

Exercises, and the early Society of Jesus which grew out of them, were a most powerful instrument for renewal in the Church. After his death, later Jesuit General Congregations began to make changes, which the *Constitutions* allowed for, as the need arose. These later Congregations began to determine by law universal norms for the spiritual life of Jesuits, for example one hour of meditation daily, daily Mass, an annual retreat. These regulations, opposed by Ignatius in his own lifetime, became the criteria for a Jesuit vocation. Retreats began to be made in groups, sometimes five hundred at a time. Different people were not allowed to have different needs; and the Exercises, consequently, no longer produced their extraordinary results. They began to be used to buttress whatever we happened to be doing. We are now living in a time of much more rapid change. Old structures, formerly accepted assumptions, in the Church and in society, are being questioned, found wanting, and swept aside. The Exercises, too, have been questioned; but the questioning has uncovered forgotten truths, which speak to us in the confusion of our times.

Jesuit Schools and the Apostolate to the Unbeliever

'I SUPPOSE YOU REALISE you're wasting your time: half of us are atheists.' This remark was addressed to me at the end of a religious education class by a sixteen-year-old pupil in a Jesuit college. However, this paper does not offer solutions to the faith problems of Catholic pupils in our Jesuit schools. Instead, I shall propose some questions on the purpose of our Jesuit educational apostolate today.

Teachers in Jesuit colleges are usually busy people, so busy that we are easily irritated by the outsider who asks, 'What is the justification for your apostolate in this school?' Recently I was a member of a working party discussing the future of a Jesuit college. As we were all very busy people, we formulated our questions quickly and found instant answers. We asked: 'Does this college answer a need? Does it answer it well?' We answered: 'There are two applicants for every available place, so we are answering a need. Our public examination record is relatively good, many of the professional men in the City are former pupils, besides a large number of priests and not a few bishops. So we are answering the need well.'

We were all too busy to examine the assumptions implicit in our questions and answers. If there is a need, does it follow that we should try to answer it? What criteria have we for choosing ministries? When we say that our examination results are relatively good, why do we elect this criterion for assessing the value of our educational apostolate? When we point to professional men, bishops and priests as evidence of a need well answered, by what standard are we assessing our apostolate? If the answers to the questions had been, 'We have a large number of empty places in our school, we have a miserable record in public examinations, more of our former pupils are in prison than in the professions and more are unemployed than employed', would it necessarily follow that we should abandon the school?

In his meditation on the Two Standards in the *Spiritual Exercises*, St Ignatius contrasts the strategy of Satan with the strategy of Christ. Satan instructs his demons to go out over the whole world 'so that no province, no place, no state of life, no individual is overlooked' (Exx 141) — and goads them on to lay snares for men and bind them with chains. First they are to tempt them to covet riches, that they may the more easily attain the empty honours of this world and then come to overweening pride. The first step, then, will be riches, the second honour, the third pride. Christ, on the other hand, instructs all his servants and friends to help all men — first to the highest spiritual poverty and even to actual poverty. Secondly they should lead men to a desire for insults and contempt, for humility springs from these.

Therefore, on these criteria, is it possible that the school with the good examination results and successful former pupils should be closed, while the school with its former pupils in prison or unemployed should continue?

In the Jesuit *Constitutions*, Ignatius gives the criteria we should use in choosing apostolates. One criterion is:

> The more universal the good is, the more it is divine. Therefore preference ought to be given to those persons and places which, through their own improvement, become a cause which can spread the good accomplished to many others who are under their influence or take guidance from them.[1]

Ignatius accepted the education of lay students as a Jesuit apostolate in the hope that these pupils would then go out and spread Christ's Kingdom. The early Jesuits had something new to offer in education and they were answering a need which no one else could answer at that particular time. Ignatius was a man of his time.

---

[1] *The Constitutions of the Society of Jesus*, translated by George E. Ganss (St Louis: Institute of Jesuit Sources, 1970), VII. 2. D [622].

The spread of Christ's Kingdom was the spread of the Roman Catholic Church and the return of the heretics to the one true fold. Government was monarchic and society was organized hierarchically. In these circumstances to educate Catholic youth who were likely to be in positions of influence later was in accordance with Ignatius' criterion, 'the more universal the good is, the more it is divine'.

Yet even in the seventeenth century Jesuits could conceive of schools which were not for Catholics only. In 1687 the Jesuits opened a school in Edinburgh. The following quotations are from its charter.

> Rules of the schools of the Royal College at Holyrood House ... scholars shall be taught gratis .... These schools are common to all, of what condition soever, and none shall be excluded .... And although youths of different professions, whether Catholic or Protestant, come to these schools, yet in teaching all there shall be no distinction made, but all shall be taught with equal diligence and care, and everyone shall be promoted according to his deserts. There shall not be, either by masters or scholars, any tampering or meddling to persuade anyone from the profession of his own religion; but there shall be all freedom for everyone to practise what religion he shall please, and none shall be less esteemed or favoured for being of a different religion from others. None shall upbraid or reproach anyone on account of religion; and when any exercise of religion shall be practised, as hearing Mass, catechizing or preaching, or any other, it shall be lawful for any Protestant, without any molestation or trouble, to absent himself from such public exercise if he pleases ....[2]

In Britain today there are six Jesuit schools: three of them are fee-paying; all six are, with a very few exceptions, for Catholics only. Are we convinced that in today's very changed circumstances we are following Ignatius' maxim 'the more universal the good is, the more it is divine', by continuing to run these six schools in the same manner as before?

---

[2] Quoted in 'The Jesuits in Scotland', *Letters and Notices*, 65 (November 1960).

St Ignatius was a missionary at heart. In the Two Standards meditation he pictures Christ sending his servants and friends to all men. Ignatius sent the early Jesuits to all men, to India, Japan, Africa, America, even to Ireland. In Europe the majority of men were either Catholic or Protestant. Ignatius sent his men to both. Nadal, who knew Ignatius so well, wrote that the Spiritual Exercises can be given not only to Catholics, but also to Protestants and even to pagans, provided they believe in one God.

We live in twentieth-century Britain, which is said to be post-Christian. Catholics form 10 per cent of the total population. Our history has tended to make us a conservative Church, more intent on preserving our faith than on spreading it. We appear to the non-Catholic as a Church with a discipline (Sunday Mass and no contraception or abortion) rather than a Church with a vision. Men and women in Britain today are hungering for a spirituality, for a meaning to life. The Youth Revolution of the 1960s and early 1970s was a cry for meaning, for a spirituality. The Catholic Church, as outsiders see it, has no answer to offer to their needs and questions. The 32nd Jesuit General Congregation of 1975, in its decree on mission, states,

> Too often we are insulated from any real contact with unbelief and with the hard consequences of injustice and oppression. As a result, we run the risk of not being able to hear the cry for the gospel as it is addressed to us by the men and women of our time.[3]

Busily engaged in running our own colleges for Catholic pupils in Britain, we can very easily become deaf and blind to the needs of our time.

---

[3] General Congregation 32, 'Our Mission Today', *The Way Supplement*, 29–30, (Spring 1977), 28.

The 32nd General Congregation states, 'The gospel demands a life free from egoism, and self-seeking and from all attempt to exploit one's fellow men'.[4] The Jesuit General, Fr Pedro Arrupe, in a speech given to Jesuit former pupils, said,

> Today our prime educational objective must be to form men-for-others, men who will live not for themselves, but for God and his Christ, for the God-man lived and died for all the world; men who cannot even conceive of the love of God which does not include love for the least of their neighbours, men completely convinced that love of God which does not issue in justice is a farce …. This kind of education goes directly counter to the prevailing educational trend everywhere in the world. First, let me ask you this question. Have we Jesuits educated you for justice? If the terms 'Justice' and 'education for Justice' carry all the depth of meaning which the Church gives them, we have not educated you for justice.[5]

In our Jesuit schools in Britain, are we educating our pupils for justice? What are we to do? More emphasis on the Third World, on voluntary service in the immediate neighbourhood of the school? I believe we are called to something much more radical.

What is involved in this 'education for Justice'? It is not simply a question of information, although information is essential, about the relation of the first two worlds to the third. Information on its own does not change attitudes. We have been bombarded with information in the media about the Third World for the last ten years, but the gap between wealthy and poor countries has widened. Within our own country we have had lots of information about the fate of the homeless, but the numbers of homeless have increased. The problem is much deeper than factual ignorance and the root of the problem is not in the Third World. It is with us in Britain and it is within each

---

[4] 'Our Mission Today', 23.
[5] Pedro Arrupe, *Men for Others* (Rome: Press and Information Office, 1973).

of us. It is a problem of the heart as well as of the head. Our heads are over-educated, our hearts and our feelings neglected, and so we cannot relate humanly to each other. We take it for granted in our education that competition is a good thing, 'brings the best out of a boy'. Yes, it certainly can do so, but often at the expense of another boy's dignity. Wealth and status are the rewards for winning. These rewards do spur men on to achieve, but they can also corrupt them, and corrupt society. Jesuit schools are inevitably caught up in this system.

Secondary education in Britain is controlled, organized and directed not according to children's needs or to the needs of the community, but by the demands of an examination system. Schools, teachers and pupils are assessed, and so come to assess themselves, against their results in public examinations, which give entrance for the privileged few to universities and colleges of further education. Therefore the majority of pupils are judged, and so judge themselves, to be educational failures. The more sensitive child is educated in diffidence, the less sensitive reacts with sullen non-cooperation or, in extreme cases, with violence. I am not suggesting that all examination systems should be abolished, still less saying that academic excellence is unimportant, but I am saying that an education which emphasizes the head at the expense of the heart and feelings, which so emphasizes the importance of examination success that children come to assess themselves and each other on this criterion, and an education which so stresses competition that children are encouraged to beat rather than to cooperate with each other, is a system which nurtures greed. If we take justice seriously then we cannot run our own schools in accordance with that system. We live in a society which accepts competition uncritically and so we have a society which favours the strong and able, while the weak suffer. We call this system 'freedom' and justify our independent schools in the name of 'freedom of choice'. An English boy, educated in China until the age of fourteen and then educated in England, was asked to comment on the two systems. 'In China', he answered 'we were taught to cooperate with each other. In England we are taught to compete against each other and to help each other is considered cheating.'

Alvin Toffler, in his book *Future Shock*, says that tomorrow's illiterate will not be the man who cannot read; he will be the man who has not learnt to unlearn.[6] To face future shock, children must be taught to be more adaptable, able to learn and unlearn, and, above all, they will require a deep inner life, self-knowledge and a strong self-identity if they are to survive future shock.

So far I have suggested that our schools should be open to non-Catholics, should go against the prevailing trend in education by emphasizing cooperation rather than competition, and should aim to prepare pupils against future shock.

St Ignatius' Annotations, preliminary observations to the *Spiritual Exercises*, contain educational principles which, if taken seriously, could revolutionise our educational methods. The early Jesuits were innovators, were accused of being excessively humanist and became the educators of Catholic Europe. They were men steeped in the Exercises. They experimented and took risks. Later generations of Jesuits became established, took a vicarious delight in the achievements of their predecessors, remained faithful to the methods and customs of old, but did not discern the signs of the times. Jesuit educators were no longer innovators, but traditionalists. Supporters of Jesuit schools in Britain today will claim that the teaching is usually methodical and thorough, that Jesuit schools are good for getting the best out of the average boy and that 'they teach a boy discipline', by which they mean that the boy will have to learn to obey rules and regulations, otherwise he will be punished. Some supporters will claim that the religious education is good. No one would accuse our colleges of being exciting, of pioneering educational

---

[6] Alvin Toffler, *Future Shock* (London: Pan, 1973).

methods, of being innovators, of being imaginative, yet the *Spiritual Exercises* contain principles which could revolutionise education.

In the Second Annotation, Ignatius warns the director against burdening the retreatant with too much information.

> The one who explains to another the method and order of meditating and contemplating should narrate accurately the facts of the contemplation or meditation. Let him adhere to the points, and add only a short or summary explanation. The reason for this is that when one in meditating takes the solid foundation of the facts and goes over it and reflects on it for himself, he may find something that makes them a little clearer or better understood .... Now this produces greater spiritual relish and fruit than if the one giving the Exercises had explained and developed the meaning at great length. For it is not much knowledge which fills and satisfies the soul, but the intimate understanding and relish of the truth. (Exx 2)

'Let them discover for themselves' is a summary of this Annotation. We Jesuits ignored its truth for centuries, when we abandoned the individually directed retreat in favour of the collective 'preached retreat'. We forgot it, too, in education, while the secular world discovered it. I know of a primary school in a very depressed city area, where discipline was the major problem and corporal punishment the only answer, until a new headmaster arrived who took the principle 'let them discover for themselves' seriously, and the school was transformed. The problem was no longer how to make the children work, but how to get them to stop working, and there was no need for corporal punishment. Secondary school teachers recognise the truth of this principle, but claim that it is impossible in practice. It would demand major changes in the administration of the school, would put strain on teachers who have not been trained for this kind of education and it would be unfair to the pupils to jeopardize their examination chances by experimenting with new methods. Our own Jesuit schools are in the same difficulty. We can acknowledge the truth of the principle 'let them discover for themselves', but we cannot practise it except in a very limited way. If this is our conclusion, do we really believe the principle? It is basic to the Exercises, basic to our belief in human freedom and human dignity. Where are our priorities?

In the Fourth Annotation, Ignatius describes how the Exercises are divided into four parts, or 'weeks', but he warns the director that some people may take a longer time, some a shorter time over each stage, and that some should not go beyond the First Week. There is no virtue, in Ignatius's mind, in covering the syllabus. How life could be enriched if we really took this principle seriously, giving priority to the needs of the individual pupil rather than to the needs of his parents, the good name of the school, the demands of the examination system. A. S. Neill, in his book *Summerhill*, says that, as a headmaster, he was happier to produce a contented road sweeper than a neurotic scholar. Ignatius would have agreed with him. Can we really put this principle into practice in our schools as we have them today?

In the Fifth Annotation, Ignatius gives the basic attitudes required in any person who wants to make the Exercises with profit. They are also the basic attitudes for openness to God, to men and to life. 'It will be very profitable for the one who is to go through the Exercises to enter upon them with magnanimity and generosity toward his Creator and Lord.' (Exx 5) In all our Christian education we must try to create the conditions 'most favourable for eliciting those qualities of magnanimity and generosity which are in us'. They are basic human qualities, to be caught rather than taught. The most lasting lessons in school are not learnt in the classroom but in the values which are absorbed almost unconsciously, by a kind of osmosis. For example, if the best teachers are always allocated to the brightest pupils, the school soon gets the message that it is brains which count. Prizes and marks confirm the impression that human worth is to be measured by ability to pass examinations. I heard a

Jesuit pupil give his mother a run-down on the personalities in his school photograph. 'He's terrifically brainy and always gets top marks. He's an absolute dud and gets everything wrong. He's pretty dim but spends hours on his homework.' The speaker then retired to his room to write out the beatitudes ten times, a punishment inflicted for his poor performance in catechism that morning. Is it practical to structure a school in such a way that the headmaster really is the servant of his staff and pupils and parents, the staff really are the servants of the pupils and the pupils learn to serve each other? Is it possible to have a school in which prefects have no privileges, senior members of staff have extra responsibility but no corresponding increment in salary, in which teaching staff, caretakers, cleaners all enjoy the same status. 'Anyone who wants to be great among you must be your servant.' (Matthew 20:26) The only school I have ever heard of which tried to put these ideas into practice was a non-Christian school.

At the heart of the Spiritual Exercises is Ignatius' belief that God acts on us through our feelings and emotions and that it is through discernment of these that we can come to know who God is and who we are. To repress and stifle these emotions is to dehumanise ourselves, cripple our spiritual powers and so silence God. Does our system of education, the administration and organization of our schools, encourage pupils and staff to be in touch with their own feelings and emotions? Do we create the atmosphere of mutual trust and acceptance in which this is possible, or do the stress and strain of school life make us consider this question a piece of idealist nonsense? We must get on with the job of helping our pupils 'to get on', keep a stiff upper lip and a smile on our face, even though there are tears in our hearts, and teach them to do the same. What kind of school would we run if we really believed that the most important thing which any of us can learn is to love and be loved, to respect the other simply because he is a human being and to be at one with him so that his pain is my pain, his joy is mine? Would it be a school with its own separate buildings and professional teaching staff, or can we envisage a school where all the community feel responsible for the children in some way, where the children can learn from the postman, the milkman, the carpenter, the mechanic, as well as from the university graduate?

I conclude with two practical suggestions. The first is that those who are engaged in teaching in our Jesuit schools should ask themselves, both individually and as a community, whether they are convinced that their work is in accord with the Exercises, the criteria for choosing ministries given in the *Constitutions*, the ideals expressed in the 32nd General Congregation and in Fr Arrupe's letters. The answer to that question is not to be found in the reasons that we adduce for or against what we are doing. The beginnings of an answer are to be found in the feelings and emotions which we experience, especially when we pray and discuss the question, and it is these feelings that we must learn to discern. Secondly, I suggest that a few Jesuits should be found, interested in the educational apostolate, who would be willing to live together in some city and work in separate state comprehensive schools, including non-Catholic schools. We cannot speak to the confusion of our times unless we share in it. Living together, they can pray and reflect together on their experience, share it in conversation and in writing with other Jesuits engaged in our own schools, and with other teachers. Working in state comprehensives which they do not control nor enjoy any privileged status in, they will feel frustration and helplessness, an important spiritual experience. Perhaps in the end they will conclude that the only way in which we can contribute anything to education in Britain is by running our own schools. On the other hand, they may experience what the early Jesuits experienced when they launched themselves into apparently impossible situations following the criterion, 'the more universal the good is, the more it is divine'. They found that the result of their work seemed quite out of proportion to the means they employed. 'Unless you lose your life, you cannot find it.' (Luke 9:24) So I pray that some of us can leave our own colleges and 'have the humility and courage to walk with the poor' and 'learn from what they have to teach us what we can do to help them'.[7]

---

[7] 'Our Mission Today', 31.

Formation for Freedom

'O FREEDOM, what liberties are taken in your name'; and the title of this paper is one such, for it suggests that men and women can be formed into a predetermined state called 'freedom', provided they do what we tell them. We can try to encourage, persuade, cajole others into accepting our way to freedom; and we may even succeed in making them conform, but in doing so we rob them of their freedom.

Man is called to freedom because he is called beyond himself to share in God's life, the source of all freedom. God's ways are not our ways: His thoughts are not our thoughts and His Spirit breathes where He will. We can never know precisely what freedom is, we can only grow in knowledge through our experience of it. For those of us in charge of the training of religious, the question is not 'how are we to form others for freedom?', but 'how can we create conditions in which we, together with those in training, can grow in freedom?' In preparing this paper I took myself in imagination to Ignatius' scene in the meditation on the Two Standards, and joined the little demons around Lucifer's 'great throne of fire and smoke', where I listened to his advice on writing this paper and on religious formation in general. He wheezed and cackled with delight at the title I had been given, 'Formation for Freedom':

> *Splendid [he said], an excellent title. After all, formation is precisely our task, to form them with terror and lies, and so ensure that they can never glimpse the freedom which the enemy has offered them. They can be very troublesome, these creatures called religious, so it is very important that you do exactly as I tell you and form them as I have formed you.*
>
> *You will find your audience are all very enthusiastic about freedom and willing to discuss the topic and attend conferences on it. They always tend to talk most on those topics which they know least. There is no harm in fostering their enthusiasm, provided you ensure*

that they never experience freedom. The more you can whip up their enthusiasm with every lie and exaggeration you can think of, the better you can succeed in separating them from the enemy and keeping them within our control. Use lots of obscure words and quote indiscriminately in foreign languages, in order to baffle and bewilder them. Be abstract and vague in this first part of your talk. Tell them that freedom, like any other gift, can only be won by blood and sweat, fidelity, perseverance and unswerving loyalty.

I was puzzled at these words of Lucifer and unfortunately showed my surprise. His reply was incisive and to the point.

You fool, surely you know by now that truth is our best ally, provided it is only half the truth. Blood and sweat, fidelity, perseverance and unswerving loyalty are virtues for us as well as for the enemy. I myself am the personification of perseverance and loyalty to the cause, the utter destruction of man, and I expect the same sense of duty from you. You will find your religious listeners are divided into two camps, called 'progressive' and 'conservative'. The more you can encourage the division, the easier it is to infiltrate both sides. 'Divide and conquer' is a good general strategy; but here you must try to win over both factions. So tell them that your talk will be based upon the inexhaustible treasures of the Church's tradition, which is ever ancient (this should please your conservative listeners) yet ever new (which should prevent your progressives from falling asleep straight away). It is some centuries ago since you were last commissioned to work among religious, so do not be surprised at their changed appearance. They are no longer dressed, most of them, in black and white uniforms, but in spite of their varied dress, they are still bound by those vile vows of poverty, chastity and obedience. However, as you know from past experience, those vows can, with a little subtlety, be turned to our advantage. So take as your subject the three vows as ways to freedom. Begin your treatment by making your audience nervous and frightened. Remind them that to be in charge of the training of religious is an awesome responsibility, and that mistakes and carelessness in training will reap a rich harvest of disaster. Make them feel responsible not only for themselves and for their charges, but also for the whole future of their Church. The more serious and solemn you can make them about themselves, the easier your task will be, because they will become so worried and preoccupied with their own responsibilities that they will no longer trust the enemy and so become easy prey. Hammer away at the old sayings, 'A good novice makes a good religious', 'Faithfulness in little things means faithfulness in great things later', 'If they keep the rule, the rule will keep them'. Dangerous teaching, I admit, but if you do exactly as I say, you can use all this to our own advantage. If you observe that the more progressive among your audience are falling asleep at this point, throw in a few cant phrases and call it 'depth psychology'. This will win back the attention of the progressives and raise the fear level of the more conservative. Tell them that the first five years in the life of a child sets the pattern for the rest of life; so too, in religious training, the early years set the pattern for the future.

If you have followed my instructions you should have succeeded by now in making your hearers more serious about themselves, more fearful and more bewildered. This tactic is what the more enlightened military human beings call 'a softening-up operation', before moving in for the kill.

You are now ready to treat of the vows in particular. Your general tactic is to arouse their potentially dangerous enthusiasm for the vows as a means to freedom, and then channel it off by suggesting a practical course of action which will not only defuse their enthusiasm, but lead them to destroy one another.

Start with poverty; make vague assertions about the Third World, world hunger, ecology, St Francis of Assisi, needles' eyes and camels. Having worked them up, assure them that unless they live their vow of poverty they will join us for ever. To ensure that they really do so and that you do not lose them at this point, move quickly into an interpretation of poverty which will render their enthusiasm quite harmless for us and destructive for them. They must be brought to understand poverty primarily as doing without things, as economizing.

Formation for Freedom 73

Those in charge of formation must be made to feel themselves responsible for ensuring that everyone in the community observes this spartan regime in all its vigour. Remind them that their novices are weak, immature, sinful people, so that those who are in charge must exercise a very strict surveillance over them in all matters, but especially in poverty. Those in training may grumble at this strict supervision, but later these former novices will be grateful. It is important, too, that this period of early training should be spent in some isolated place where the religious may be safely insulated from the actual poverty of their fellow human beings.

If you communicate this message successfully, you will enjoy watching its destructive effects later on, both in individuals and in communities. The deprivations imposed on novices in the name of poverty, and the strict supervision by those in charge, will engender ill-feeling within the community, increase their greed and develop in them deceitfulness and dishonesty. The more rigorous the economies, the wealthier the communities are likely to become, increasing their properties, which will, in turn, demand more economies and more energy diverted into fund-raising, which is one of the most profitable occupations in which we can involve them. They will soon be ensnared in their corporate possessions.

The enforced economies within the community will lead to irritability, discontent and grumbling. Discontent is a most powerful ally for us, provided it is kept secret and not openly expressed; so you must exhort them to stifle their anger, reminding them that they must not expect the vows to be easy. Arouse their enthusiasm for poverty by any means you like, then channel this potentially dangerous enthusiasm into detailed observation of restrictive measures, practices which will irritate them and engender ill-feeling within the community. Stifle this irritation by reminding them that their grumbles are due to unfreedom and selfishness within them. These tactics should ensure a growing love of possessions, deceitfulness, mutual mistrust and moral irresponsibility. The fear level in your audience, gradually rising during your treatment of poverty, should leap up when you come to treat of chastity. Be extremely vague at first. Emphasize the delicacy of the matter which you are now going to treat, and develop this until you see that they are all thoroughly uncomfortable. Then begin to praise the virtue of chastity, subtly ensuring that they understand the virtue to mean living as though their sexuality did not exist, extol the preciousness of the gift and tell them how easily it is lost, bringing them to a state of near panic. Your tactics will be very simple. Make them afraid of their own sexuality. As this is an integral part of their nature as social beings, fear of their own sexuality makes them afraid of themselves and of friendship with each other. Justify this fear for them by assuring them that their love of God must be stronger than any human friendship. This will ensure that they do not get near to him who, in his folly, became one of them, befriended them and identifies himself with each one of them.

Speak much of love and tell them that their love is proved and improved by their getting on with the job appointed for them by superiors. Be careful that they never speak the truth about how they feel or what they think on chastity or any other matter. Frighten them into trying to live as angels like ourselves. Then they will begin to despise their bodies, hate themselves and each other, and so destroy themselves. If you should fail to destroy them with the first two vows, even incompetent idiots like yourselves should succeed in destroying them with the final vow of obedience. If you disobey my orders and fail in this, know that the torments you have suffered are as nothing in comparison with those you will endure. I cannot tolerate any disobedience in my demons. Obedience means obeying my order to the letter; this is the message you have to communicate to them. Insist that the essence of religious life consists in surrendering their will and judgment to their superior and doing exactly as they are told. Speak in praise of this virtue and of the inestimable value of obedience of their will and judgment. Remind them that they are sinful, weak, blinded in their intellects and wounded in will, twisted, unreliable, untrustworthy. Assure them that the only way to freedom is by abandoning their own will and judgment and submitting it to superiors.

Any threatened deviation from the path leading to their own destruction can easily be prevented by appeal to this virtue. If practised for long enough, they will eventually lose the ability to think or feel for themselves or for others, and become creatures whose appetite for orders is matched only by their appetite for food. Once we have reduced them to this unthinking and unfeeling state, our problems are over. We may safely leave them to their own destruction.

With a final exhortation to obedience and the threat of prolonged torture if I failed, Lucifer dismissed me in a puff of acrid smoke to prepare my paper on 'Formation for Freedom'.

In this perverted way, what am I trying to say? Briefly, that much of what passes for religious formation impoverishes the person by undermining his self-confidence and so destroying the very source of his communication with God. God dwells within us, His Spirit speaks to our spirit. If we dare not trust ourselves, we dare not trust God either. If we are afraid of ourselves, we cannot know ourselves, cannot discern what is happening within us and therefore cannot come to know God's will for us.

If the vows are to lead us to freedom, they must be chosen freely and loved for their own sake, not endured as a temporary deprivation in the hope of an eternal reward. Poverty, chastity and obedience are not the preserve of religious. Every human being is called to these virtues. In religious life we take the three vows as a means to help us to grow in these virtues.

In the remaining part of this paper I shall treat very briefly of the three vows as a means to finding freedom.

I was searching late one evening for a place in which to camp for the night. I called at a house where the owner took me to the end of his garden, pointed to a field and said, 'It's yours'. Later, I sat outside the tent, gazed over the field and said, 'It's mine'. I felt great happiness in that moment. I could enjoy the field as mine precisely because I had no claim on it, and was not worried at the thought of losing it when I moved on next morning. Afterwards, whenever I camped, wherever I rested, I used to look around at the fields and orchards, the mountains and valleys and say, 'It's mine'. In Christ I can possess all things: in myself I can only be possessed and imprisoned by what I own. I had a glimpse of the truth that in Christ I could possess all things precisely because I possessed nothing. I began to see the value of the vow of poverty. It is the vow which can help us to know that everything that we have and all that we are is a gift freely given to which we have no right. This inner knowledge heightens our appreciation and enjoyment of the material world and of every moment of existence.

Those vowed to poverty renounce material possessions. This renunciation can help us to break out of our cocoon of self-interest, not only in regard to material possessions, but from all those attachments which enclose, constrict and stifle us. Just as the field became mine on that evening precisely because it was not mine and I could let it go next day, so too with my possession of my own life. I must learn to see it as mine precisely because it is not mine: I must possess it in poverty, ready to let it go. 'Unless you lose your life, you cannot find it'; 'Blessed are the poor, for theirs is the kingdom of heaven'. The vow of poverty is practised as a means of helping us to know and experience the truth of these words of Christ.

What kind of religious training can help us to glimpse the value of poverty? Love of poverty is like any other love: it cannot be forced. We can only effect an introduction, and try to create the conditions in which this love can grow. The conditions must avoid both penury and destitution on the one hand, luxury and softness on the other.

St Ignatius devised a series of experiments for his novices which were designed to recreate the conditions in which he and his first companions had discovered their vocation. The experiments included a thirty-day retreat, corresponding to his own experience at Manresa, a month's pilgrimage on foot, begging one's way, a period of work in hospitals and time spent in teaching poor children their catechism. Today we need to devise similar experiments in which novices can have some experience of living poor with those who are poor, sharing what they have and experiencing the joy as well as the hardship of living in insecurity and uncertainty.

Perhaps we shall never succeed in devising real as distinct from artificial experiments, until we religious find ourselves without money, without property, like the founders and first members of most religious orders and congregations. Novice masters and mistresses would then have to train their charges in small groups living in poor areas, supporting themselves like any other poor family. Living in small groups in an unobtrusive way and sharing the life of the poor is more likely to enable us to glimpse the value of the virtue of poverty than living in a large building, insulated within religious walls from the life of the poor, and practising a form of poverty which, far from freeing the spirit, can make us more self-protective, possessive and timid.

Integrity is a virtue to which all men are called. Chastity is the virtue of integrity as it affects us as sexual creatures. All men are called to chastity. Some are called to it through marriage; others are called to it through celibacy/virginity. The most important element in training religious for chastity is enabling them to discover within themselves their desire for celibacy/virginity as a means to chastity. It is only in so far as we discover this desire deep within us that we are capable of ordering our emotions and appetites and withstanding the more superficial and temporary drives within us. Unless there is a genuine desire to live a celibate life, enforced celibacy can become destructive of human life and spirituality.

Chastity is a virtue which concerns our sexuality, but our sexuality pervades our whole being. Training in chastity must include forming habits of intellectual honesty and emotional sincerity. Uncritical enthusiasm for a cause, indiscriminate grumbling, sentimental piety, religious effusiveness are unchaste. Lucifer was right in saying 'You cannot exaggerate too much'. In noviceships enormous harm can be done by subjecting novices to a hothouse atmosphere of sentimental and uncritical piety. Training in honest criticism is part of training in chastity.

Chastity is the virtue which enables us to grow more at one with ourselves and with our own sexuality, and so be more wholeheartedly dedicated to Christ. A fanatical denial of sexuality is just as unchaste as concubinage. Fear of our own sexuality and refusal to acknowledge it is fear of ourselves and of the depths within us. This fear separates us from God and stifles our spiritual growth.

In training religious we must try to help novices to grow out of fear of their own sexuality. Openness, honesty and a sense of humour in discussing sexuality is essential. A training in prayer which enables novices to get in touch with their own deepest feelings is an important part of training in chastity, because in finding in their own genuine and deepest feelings a call to celibacy/virginity, they will want to be loyal to this gift in face of temporary, superficial feelings.

We grow in chastity as in any other virtue, and a rigid segregation of the sexes during the years of training can stunt growth in the virtue. But, surely, great strictness and discipline is required for training in chastity? Certainly, but the control must be the control of love. If we really want celibacy/virginity, the control must come from the wanting. Imposed precautions, excessive protection and prohibitions can weaken the novice and eventually lead to emotional childishness and irresponsibility.

All institutions, including religious ones, are potential tyrannies. The institution, very naturally, prefers the safe and predictable man. The man without ideas is unlikely to be a nuisance. If obedience is thought of as the virtue which enables the institution to run smoothly, then Christ was the most disobedient of men.

The root meaning of obedience is *obaudire*, to listen. Obedience is the virtue which enables us to listen to God in the depths of us.

He is a mysterious God who leads us beyond ourselves, to transcend ourselves to be at one with Him.

It is not easy to listen to God; listening to Him demands sacrifice. If I feel drawn to Him, He calls me to love my neighbour as myself. I must then abandon a way of life which gives priority to my own ease, my own wants and needs. If I want to achieve anything in life, I have to make sacrifices, organize the claims on me and find a priority of values. If I really want to climb mountains, I have to remove my carpet slippers, abandon the armchair and all the other counter-attractions of the day.

I am a social animal. If I am to be obedient to my truest self, I must also be obedient to others. I need them to find myself. I need to listen to them if I am to learn to listen to myself.

If authority demands obedience simply because it says so, without reference to the individual's or anyone else's good, then disobedience is the only morally responsible reply.

In obedience of will and judgment I recognise my own blindness, my own deafness. Through obedience to others I am willing to break down the barriers which enclose me in my own point of view, and so widen my vision and increase my perceptiveness, in order that I may become more perceptive and responsive to God within me. But if I abandon all trust in my own will and judgment, I also abandon my power of listening and responding to God at work within me and become spiritually dead.

Training in prayer is a vital part of training in obedience. The essence of prayer is obedience in the literal sense of the word, *obaudire*.

Those in charge of formation must be good listeners to God in prayer and to those under their care. They must also love those who are in their charge. The exercise of obedience outside a context of love and understanding is destructive.

If obedience is listening to God and to one another, there is no reason why obedience should be exercised in a subject–superior relationship rather than in a group relationship in which important decisions are discussed by all and reached by agreement. There is just as much need for obedience in a democracy as in a monarchy. Those in formation should be allowed some share in shaping it.

Developing the critical faculties of novices, far from being subversive, is an integral part of training in obedience.

If obedience is the virtue of listening and responding to God at work within us, it is important that the period of religious training should provide individuals with plenty of opportunity to exercise their own initiative and make their own mistakes, so that the training produce not character, but characters.

To sum up. I have rejected the title with which I began this paper, 'Formation for Freedom', and have tried to show that training men and women for religious life is to work in cooperation with them to discover freedom in Christ. The three vows are the traditional means to that freedom. If they are to be effective means, they must so be practised that they lead us more and more to love poverty, chastity and obedience as the virtues which answer our deepest longings.

Spiritual Development and the Directed Retreat

I GAVE MY FIRST eight-day preached retreat in 1960, setting off with a file containing 32 talks. We had been warned that we would always be thanked at the end for 'a lovely retreat, most helpful', but that the acid test came later—were we invited to give another at that house or with that congregation? I was thanked for a lovely retreat, but was not invited again to that house or to that congregation. However, I was not worried. I felt a certain security in that file of 32 talks. I continued giving two or three preached retreats annually during school vacations. The contents of the file grew, but I was beginning to feel uneasy with these retreats, an uneasiness which I found it difficult to explain at the time. I think I understand better now, over ten years later. In this paper I shall analyze the uneasiness, show the place, usefulness and limits of the preached retreat, and point out the essential differences which I think exist between a directed retreat which includes a session providing suggestions for prayer each day to the whole group, and one in which there are no such daily sessions.

My uneasiness over preached retreats was an instance of a much more general question about the nature of faith. At that time I was in contact with a variety of people of different religions and none. The goodness I saw in them, integrity of life, openness to truth, fair-mindedness, concern for others did not, in general, correspond to any particular religious belief or practice. I also saw dishonesty, refusal to face truth, lack of concern for others in people who were practising Christians. I could not dismiss this fact by reminding myself that I am a sinner in a Church of sinners. It seemed to me that the way in which religion is presented and practised can foster closed attitudes, shield us from experience, encourage cowardice in the face of truth, bolster up the individual and foment group selfishness. 'Thank you for a lovely retreat' could mean 'Thank you for not disturbing me and justifying me in my present way of life'. I was beginning to see more clearly the danger of living inside a cocoon of religiosity, comfortable as long as I could be unaware that I was in a cocoon, the danger of domesticating God, interpreting His word in such a way that it could reinforce the cocoon, sheltering me from the true God, from the truth of my own experience and from 'the tears of things'.

I still see this danger in myself and I see it in the Church, among the clergy, religious orders and congregations, and among the laity. There are notable and hopeful exceptions; but as a body of Christians, the Catholic Church in Britain does spend an inordinate amount of time and energy on itself and its own survival, on maintenance rather than on mission, even to its own lapsed members. Christ spoke of leaving the ninety-nine to search for the one that was lost. In the Church in Britain the proportion of Catholics who still practise their religion is less than 50 per cent, but there is no organized apostolate, as far as I know, to those who have ceased practising. In saying this, I am not, of course, saying that those who are no longer practising are lost, but many of them are hungering for spiritual help. Ecumenically, we have progressed at the theological level in the last twenty years; but at present there is little sign of any general ecumenical interest or activity. Yet the unity of Christians is Christ's will. Somehow we have cocooned ourselves against it. There are few indications of serious attempts to explain Christianity in a language which non-religious people can understand, yet Christ died for all men and his message is for all men. The Catholic response to political issues tends to be very selective—abortion and Catholic schools. Increasing unemployment, harsher immigration laws, increased expenditure on what is euphemistically called 'defence' and decreased expenditure on overseas aid do not elicit any united response from the Catholic body.

The problem I am considering is not an inner church problem. It is much wider than that. As a nation we have an excellent educational system, social services, national health service and communications media which penetrate almost every home. For years we have been flooded with information and analysis on housing problems, third-world problems, the dangers of nuclear warfare and so on; but the problems worsen. Somehow the knowledge fails to transform the mind and heart, and so fails to result in any effective action.

The question which was at the root of the uneasiness that I experienced in giving eight-day preached retreats is this: how does real change take place within the human mind and heart? One way is through the individually given retreat; but that, too, can be ineffective in many cases, even where there is good will on the part of the retreatant and a skilled director. The environment in which we live, our life-style, the people with whom we associate, the work we do, may influence us so strongly that there is no hope of inner change unless there is also a change in these environmental influences, either before or after the retreat.

Spiritual development is a slow and gradual process of growth in our consciousness of who we are. The child does not ask the question; the adolescent begins to ask it and may even find an answer which satisfies for a day or two; the adult begins to see the enormity of the question, is both frightened and fascinated by it, may refuse to face it and try to live in childish unawareness, or ignore the complexity of the question and seize upon some abstract explanation which suits his own way of living.

Ignatius says of the Exercises in his First Annotation:

> We call Spiritual Exercises every way of preparing and disposing the soul to rid itself of all inordinate attachments and, after their removal, of seeking and finding the will of God in the disposition of our life for the salvation of our soul.

Attachments which are ordinate at one stage of life may be inordinate at another, and there is an innate tendency in us to cling to our attachments. The umbilical chord is an ordinate attachment until we are born. A continuing attachment would bring death.

An infant spends much of its time in touching, tasting and the other sense perceptions. Such activity is vital for the child, the condition of its learning; for all knowledge begins with sense perception. A child's memory is very receptive, and it can easily pick up and relish the most complicated jingles without giving a thought to their meaning. What it is told, it accepts as true without question: a necessary characteristic of the infant. The child needs affection, stability and protection, otherwise it cannot develop. All these predominant needs and activities of childhood are ordinate. If they remain the predominant needs and activities, the child remains infantile; their predominance has become inordinate. Throughout life we always need sense perception, to have our memory stored, to be able to accept the voice of authority, to have affection, stability and protection; but these are no longer our predominant needs because others have come into play.

Religion must answer these human needs of infancy which perdure throughout life. It must speak to our senses as well as to our heads through the art, music and gesture of the liturgy. It must store our memory with its tradition, give moral and doctrinal guidance, afford a sense of stability, protect its people from danger and let them know that they are important and of great worth.

In adolescence, other activities and needs begin to predominate over the needs and activities of childhood; principally, the search for meaning and unity in experience. The adolescent begins to question in order to make sense of what he experiences, the facts with which he is presented, the statements which he formerly accepted as true. He begins to criticize, sift evidence, form theories and explanations. The explanations may be lamentable and the theories crude, but the activity is healthy and necessary for human development. We can only act as human beings if we have a reason.

Religion must answer this human need by showing the coherence of belief and experience, providing theories and hypotheses which help us to see the relationships and unity in all that we experience.

If religion fails to do this, then it will become a compartment of life, sealed off from other areas, neither affecting nor being affected by them. Religion, if it is to answer the needs of human development, must be critical, speculative, provide philosophies and theologies.

No philosophy or theology can ever be adequate to answer the questions which arise out of the mystery of our existence. Abstract theories are two-dimensional and cannot grasp the multi-dimensional nature of our inner experience. Consciousness of this inner world becomes the predominant activity in adulthood. We are essentially creatures of action, but the environment in which we live, the people we meet, the knowledge we acquire, our successes and failures, set up conflicts within us of desires, fears, anxieties, hopes. Our own actions and reactions can take us by surprise; we grow more aware of the mystery of our being, more sceptical of simple explanations. We come to know that the explanation of all our behaviour, of the way we see and evaluate people and things, the source of our energy and our lethargy, our joy and our sorrow, lies within this inner world, although we do not know how. This inner world is fascinating, but it is also frightening.

Religion must answer this adult stage with a third element, which encourages our fascination and dispels our fears of this inner world, encouraging us to enter it through the practice of prayer, assuring us that God is in the dark and labyrinthine ways of our minds, consciousness and subconscious, that we are right in thinking that the source of all our joy and sorrow, hope and despair is in this inner self, that in His light and with His help we can come to know the destructive and the life-giving forces which are deep within us, recognise the inordinate attachments and find the true source of life.

In each stage of human, and therefore also of spiritual, development, there is an innate reluctance to move on to the next stage. Each stage, while necessary, is also dangerous. What is presented to us in infancy answers our most basic needs, allows us to be relatively passive, protected and secure. The danger is that we do not want to move out of this stage and choose to remain infantile. In our spiritual development there is the same danger. Our temptation is to remain credulous, unquestioning, docile and secure; and we are opposed to any form of criticism which could jeopardize this security. The necessary element in religion which corresponds to the needs of childhood is the institutional element, which presents religion to us in ritual, passes on the tradition, teaches with authority. The temptation of those in authority in religion is to encourage this innate danger of infantilism by discouraging criticism and questioning, emphasizing the virtues of obedience, docility and loyalty, without making it clear that obedience is to God, docility to truth, and loyalty to God as made known to us in our own conscience. Infantile assent is more in the nature of a conditioned response, ordinate in the child, inordinate in the adult, because it then stifles spiritual growth.

In the adolescent critical stage of life, the danger is that this questioning may undermine the security and protection which we enjoyed in the infancy stage. We may be led to reject the traditions and teachings which we were given in childhood, become alienated from our families and friends, and possibly lose the protection and affection which we need for human growth.

In religion, the danger is that the critical element cuts adrift from the institutional and produces rationalists rather than religious people, whose devotion to a system of philosophy or theology will take the place of their devotion to God. Such people will be suspicious of anything emotional, subjective or devotional. If the critical element is not balanced and held in tension by the other two elements, it will produce followers who are incapable of communicating with the child in themselves, or with any other child; they cut out communication with their own inner world, which is far too complex adequately to be described in abstract concepts.

In the adult, the danger is that we become so absorbed in this inner world, its mystery and power, that we reject the institutional element in life and religion, reject the traditions we have received and the authority we once accepted; whilst we despise all abstract philosophies and theologies as totally inadequate to describe the richness of the reality we have found within.

In religion, if this inner element, the mystical element, is emphasized to the exclusion of the institutional and critical, this can lead to a rejection of formal prayer and ritual, to abandonment of doctrinal and moral teaching, and to an emotionalism which is not understood because it will not submit itself to any critical analysis. In its worst forms, the mystical element can produce wild enthusiasts, dangerous and autocratic fanatics.

In the remainder of this paper I shall apply this analysis to the giving of retreats. Real change takes place within the human heart through our coming to know our inner selves in the light of God's goodness. We are afraid to do this, and have many and devious defence systems to protect ourselves against truth. 'The heart is more devious than any other thing, perverse, too: who can pierce its secrets?' (Jeremiah 17:9) What method of retreat-giving is the more likely to help us to enter our inner selves and uncover our deviousness?

A preached retreat, of its nature, must be an exercise of the institutional element of religion. It may include a greater or lesser emphasis on the critical element, depending on the audience, and an encouragement to move into the 'mystical'. The preached retreat is instructional, even if the material offered is designed not to fill with knowledge, but to offer a more intimate understanding of the truth. It has its place in spiritual development for beginners. Repeated annually throughout life, it becomes burdensome for those who are developing spiritually; and it may encourage those who are not to remain where they are. For those who are going through a predominantly critical stage in their spiritual development, a preached retreat can be agony, as they sit in enforced silence listening to statements which they want to question or can no longer accept. When the mind is in turmoil, it is difficult to pray.

For those who have not allowed themselves to enter the critical, questioning stage in religious development, a preached retreat annually will not be particularly burdensome, because they are habitually passive in religious matters and have not searched to find a coherence in their own lives between what they experience and what they believe. They still tend to overemphasize God's transcendence in their prayer and thinking, and to neglect His immanence. God is their all, but He is not in all. They will make clear distinctions in their thinking and in their behaviour between the sacred and the secular, the natural and the supernatural. In private prayer they will strive for a prayer which is without images, thought or feeling; and the blankness they experience they can attribute to the dark night of the soul. Their preference will be for prayer in common, liturgical celebration, set forms, even mantras. In their spiritual development they will move from the institutional to the mystical stage, avoiding the critical. Their religious lives will reflect their prayer: they will be sealed off from ordinary life. The word does not become flesh.

The most helpful form of retreat for those who are developing spiritually is the individually directed. The third stage in human development I have called the mature stage; but 'mature' is a very relative word. It means that stage in life when the needs and activities of infancy and adolescence are no longer predominant, and when we become increasingly aware of our own inner life and its complexities. It is not mature in the sense that we have arrived at our inner destination and are now fully integrated. The mature person is more aware than the child or the adolescent of his own ignorance, of the inadequacy of his own mind to grasp, explain and understand what he experiences. A fourth-century writer describes the state well: 'Blessed is he who has reached the state of utter ignorance; his is the kingdom of heaven'; but in his ignorance he knows that this mysterious inner world is the source of his life, of his freedom and enslavement. He now understands better the meaning of Christ's teaching that it is not what goes into a man from the outside which causes uncleanness.

In this inner world each of us is unique; no one else can experience it as I experience it. It is hard to communicate it even to ourselves, because language is always inadequate; yet unless we do try to formulate the experience in words, we cannot interpret what is happening. The temptation is always to ignore what is happening, pretend that it is not there, anaesthetize ourselves in some way. Drink or drugs are one way, but there are many other less physically harmful ways: intense busyness with work or hobbies, any form of distraction which will keep the inner demons at bay. But the words of Horace the Roman poet remain true: *Naturam expellas furca, tamen usque recurret* ('if you drive out nature with a pitchfork, she will soon find a way back').

Inner transformation takes place when we enter this inner world, allow what is within our consciousness and subconscious to surface by putting ourselves in the presence of the God of all goodness who has given Himself to us in Christ, entered our darkness and overcome all the destructive powers within and around us.

In the Second Annotation to the *Spiritual Exercises*, Ignatius writes:

> Let him [the giver of the Exercises] adhere to the points and add only a short or summary explanation. Now this produces greater spiritual relish and fruit than if one giving the Exercises had explained and developed the meaning at great length. For it is not much knowledge which fills and satisfies the soul, but the intimate understanding and relish of the truth.

The process, then, is to introduce a topic for prayer as briefly as possible and then let the retreatant discover for himself. Too lengthy an explanation can be an obstacle to this inner discovery. There is a natural tendency in us to shirk the inner journey; and lengthy explanations by a retreat-giver can provide us with a convenient escape, as we follow the contortions of his thought and so avoid ourselves.

In the Fourth Annotation, Ignatius warns that some are slower than others in attaining what is sought. Once a retreatant begins to discover for himself, he will know when he is ready to move on. To rush him or force him through set exercises at a prescribed pace is to interfere with the whole process of inner understanding. That is why I think that giving a set talk each day to a group of retreatants, even although they are also interviewed individually, is a radically different process from seeing them individually and having no talk to the group, so that each may go at his own pace. Those retreatants who may tend to be stuck in the institutional stage will not be helped by a directed retreat in which there are prescribed scripture passages for each day for all. They may be only too glad to move on quickly from topic to topic. I think it is this danger which Ignatius has in mind when he writes in the Eleventh Annotation:

> While the exercitant is engaged in the first week of the Exercises, it will be helpful if he knows nothing of what is to be done in the second week. Rather, let him labour to attain what he is seeking in the first week, as if he hoped to find no good in the second.

Those whose spiritual development is still predominantly in the critical stage will almost certainly find something in the daily talk to argue about with themselves or with the director, so that the daily talks will be an obstacle to prayer for them. Those who are not stuck in the institutional critical stage would do well to absent themselves from the talks altogether. It is also very difficult to see how a retreat which includes one talk per day to the whole group, providing prayer material for the day, can be in accordance with the Eighteenth Annotation:

> The Spiritual Exercises must be adapted to the conditions of the one who is to engage on them: that is, to his age, education and talent. Thus exercises that he could not easily bear, or from which he would deprive no profit, should not be given to one with little natural ability or of little physical

Spiritual Development and the Directed Retreat

strength. Similarly, each one should be given those exercises that would be more helpful and profitable according to his willingness to dispose himself for them.

The most common obstacle to spiritual development is a fear which is not conscious but which effectively blocks our ability to pray, our familiarity with God and our freedom in action. As the fear is not conscious, it will take time to surface. Until it does surface, Christ's yoke becomes more difficult and his burden heavier. Symptoms of this fear are sometimes indicated by a retreatant who remains in a state of constant euphoria and for whom every prayer experience is 'beautiful'. Other indications may be prayer which is imageless, thoughtless, in a retreatant who finds human relations difficult and has never known friendship. When these symptoms show themselves, then certain scripture passages and gospel contemplations are more likely to draw the fears into consciousness than others; this often happens in repetitions when in the first attempt to pray the passage the retreatant was unable to get anything out of it. In a directed retreat which offers all retreatants the same subject matter each day, unconscious fears, if they exist, are less likely to surface.

More important than the selection of apt scripture passages is the retreat-giver's ability to face his own fears. If he is not doing so, his fear will be communicated unconsciously to the other person, thus steering the retreatant away from those areas of experience which the director cannot cope with himself. This can happen without his being conscious of what he is doing. For example, he can be very forceful and vehement in the advice he gives, hurry on the retreatant to another contemplation, take refuge in funny anecdotes, and so on. If the one who is giving the Exercises finds himself repeating the same texts and saying the same things to each retreatant, then he cannot be listening to them—possibly because he is afraid to do so.

Another common obstacle to spiritual growth is our inability to forgive. This can be so deep as to be beyond our consciousness;

yet it still has a stifling effect on our spiritual growth. 'He who is forgiven little, loves little'; and also, presumably, forgives little. If I am not conscious of having been forgiven, I am not free to forgive or to take risks. I therefore have to protect myself, assure myself and be assured. Like fear, this inability to forgive acts as a restrictive block within us, and exhortations to a more generous following of Christ simply act as an additional burden. This awareness of our need to forgive may take a long time to surface.

False notions of spirituality generally, and of the meaning of God's will in particular, can also stunt our spiritual growth. If God's will is thought of as a blueprint, extrinsic to my inner desires, then my innermost self will never consent to it. It will remain buried, while I consent with another 'holy' self, which is not true, not rooted in the depths of me. I can justify myself in this with odd snatches of spiritual reading about the death of the self and of all desires, and so on. I assume a holy and devout persona during the time of retreat and of prayer, but it will not last. If we have false notions of God's will and our consent is not deep-rooted, this will show itself in the nature of the consolation and desolation we experience. Desolation will feel real enough; but consolation will not have that feeling of reality and genuineness. It will feel false, we shall be afraid of its disappearing too quickly; nor will it change our attitudes or actions once the retreat is over.

Unless I come to desire God's will in the roots of my being, I cannot be wholehearted in prayer and action. That is why Ignatius emphasizes desire so much in the Exercises. 'Our one desire and choice should be what is more conducive to the end for which we are created'. This statement of the 'Principle and Foundation' runs through the Exercises: 'I should ask for what I desire'. 'Thou hast created us for thyself, and our heart is restless until it rests in thee', as Augustine wrote at the beginning of his *Confessions*. If we could find what we really desire in the depth of ourselves, we would have discovered God's will. Then we would genuinely desire to be dead to our false, superficial selves. It may take a retreatant a long time to discover this truth (for example, by many repetitions of the contemplation of Christ asking John's disciples, 'what do you want?', John 1:35–39). Once discovered, this truth gives great inner freedom and confidence in the presence of Christ dwelling and working in our inner being. There is, obviously, a better chance of coming to this truth in an individually given retreat, in which the retreatant is allowed to go at his own pace.

After the phrase 'I should ask for what I desire', Ignatius goes on: 'Here it will be to pray for ——'. Do I pray for what I desire, or for what I should desire; and is there not a contradiction in praying for what I should desire? In working with teams of retreat-givers, and at conferences on the Exercises, the question is often asked, 'How do you know when someone is ready to move on in the Exercises?'; and the answer is given equally often: 'have they received the grace of the week or the day?' I am unhappy with this answer. If I am told often enough and strongly enough that 'this is what you should desire', my devious soul can get it, but by means of a kind of transference; and my real self is not in touch with the desire. I find that most retreatants, new to the Exercises, if told to pray for what they desire, and asked afterwards what they did pray for, have, in fact, prayed for those things which the text of the *Exercises* says they should desire.

The greatest and most common obstacle to spiritual development is a deep-rooted self-distrust, which can often masquerade as humility. Spiritual language is full of ambiguity. There is a sense in which it is true that we should distrust ourselves; but it is also true that a basic distrust in ourselves must necessarily include distrust in God, who can only communicate Himself through our listening selves. If I am to find God in all things, I must find Him within my own self, within its darkness as well as in its light. The most radical ecumenism is ecumenism within our own psyche. It is only in so far as we are able to accept ourselves that we are able to accept others.

If there is a basic self-distrust, then we cannot recognise consolation when it comes. If it does come, then the distrusting self immediately suspects it, disregards it, and so effectively cuts off communication with God.

To return to some of the questions asked at the beginning of this paper: why is ecumenism so dead in most areas of Britain? Why are we a Catholic Church more concerned with her own inner church affairs than with the world she is meant to serve? Why is she so negligent of her own lapsed members, so lacking in missionary zeal, so incapable of speaking to the unbeliever in a language he can begin to understand? The root of the problem lies within our own inner self, which is unwilling to confront and communicate with the questioning, fearful, doubting, anxious, diffident, unbelieving part of itself. Until we become willing, inner transformation cannot take place. I have tried to show the limits and possibilities in various forms of retreat giving, concluding that the form of retreat most likely to bring about this inner change is the individually given retreat, presented strictly according to Ignatius' Annotations, and therefore excluding any talk to the retreatants as a group, in which the same prayer material is given to all for each day.

[In April 1979, eighteen Jesuits and six religious women engaged in retreat work met at St Beuno's, to discuss the future of the house as a Centre of Jesuit Spirituality. The first session was on the ambiguity of the term 'directed retreat'; and examples were cited of a bewildering variety of spiritual activities which are currently being advertised as 'directed retreats'. It soon became clear that there was also ambiguity in the use of the term among those who were present at the meeting. Most understood it to mean a retreat in which there was opportunity for individual direction, but the retreat giver would talk to the retreatants as a group each day and provide them with scripture passages and other material for the prayer of that day. For others, a directed retreat must be conducted individually without any talk being given to the whole group. We realised that a full discussion

of this topic would take up the whole of our two-day meeting and decided to hold a later conference on the directed retreat. It was then discovered that the Irish Province Jesuits had decided to hold a conference on the same subject. When England and Ireland agree independently, the hand of God is obviously there.

This paper originated in a talk given at the joint English–Irish conference, held in January 1980. Ed.]

Spiritual Direction and the Priest

IF ASKED 'do you consider receiving regular spiritual direction to be important in the life of a priest?', diocesan bishops and religious provincials are unlikely to answer, 'No, and that is why I have never made provision for it in my diocese/congregation'. Yet I do not know of any diocese or religious order which, until very recent years, made any serious provision for regular spiritual direction for its priests, or provided any specialised training for spiritual directors. For years men would study to qualify as lecturers in canon law, moral or dogmatic theology; and seminarians would spend six or seven years learning from these men as part of their preparation for priesthood. Spiritual directors, however, had no such training; and spirituality, the source of all theology, if treated at all, was given a very minor place. In my own four years' study of theology we had one course (I think it lasted for one semester) called 'ascetical theology'. The weekly session was nicknamed 'Holy Hour', looked upon as a period of light relaxation and, because there was no examination at the end of it, many of us did not bother to attend.

In most seminaries and religious houses of studies there would be a man with the title 'spiritual father'. Arrangements might differ from place to place, but I think it is fair to say that usually men were appointed to such a post when they no longer had the energy for anything else. They were chosen for their piety and friendliness rather than any gift of learning or skill in discernment. Consequently, spiritual direction was experienced as a minor chore to be endured in order to keep the old boy happy rather than as a time of clarification, enlightenment and encouragement. My own memories of many years of such spiritual direction can be reduced in their essential content to a few brief questions and answers:

Himself: *Well now, how are you?*
Myself: *Fine, thanks, Father.*

Himself: *Well, that's good. And the prayer—how are you finding the prayer?*

Myself: *I try, but I don't have much success. My mind runs all over the place.*

Himself: *Yes, we all find it difficult, but the most important thing is that you persevere and keep praying. Nobody can pretend it's easy.*

The essentials were then over. The remainder of the time would be spent in discussion, the topic depending on the spiritual father of that time. It might be sport, or a little bit of house gossip or, in one case, the role of the machine-gunner in the major battles of the Great War, in which Father had served as a sergeant! There was one occasion when I told the spiritual father that I was being tormented with doubts about faith. I have never forgotten his reaction. 'Oh my God', he exclaimed, and then asked me if I was sure that I had not been neglecting prayer. It took me many years and much pain before I was able to understand what was happening in these doubts. A good spiritual director would have shown no sign of shock and could have let me talk freely about what I was experiencing, thus helping me to see the difficulties as an invitation to grow in faith.

The art of spiritual direction had been lost and in its place was a benevolent system for checking up on student priests to see that they were 'doing' their spiritual duties and that they had someone to talk to if they had difficulties of conscience. It is not surprising that bishops and provincials did not consider spiritual direction to be of any great importance.

In recent years there are signs of a growing awareness of the need for spiritual direction, not only for priests and religious but for every Christian. In their enthusiasm, its advocates tend to exaggerate its value. 'Absolutely vital'; 'essential for anyone who is serious about the spiritual life'; 'every priest should have a spiritual director'. The problem is that when someone asks, 'Excuse me Father, but I live in "X". Could you recommend any spiritual director within twenty miles?', the usual answer is, 'No, sorry, I can't', with the more optimistic person adding, 'but I'm sure if you look around you'll find someone eventually'. If having a spiritual director is presented as necessary for salvation, then most of the present generation of priests must resign themselves to being deprived of such means within their own lifetime!

A further question arises when talking with people who have had regular spiritual direction in their lives. I reckon that if I had kept careful record of all the conversations, I could produce a useful thesis entitled 'Spiritual Nemesis', corresponding to Ivan Illich's *Medical Nemesis*, maintaining that, often, people would have been better off if they had not had a spiritual director. The director is a very privileged person, who is allowed into the recesses of another's mind and heart. Of all the mechanisms of man and of nature, the human psyche is by far the most delicate. To blunder around insensitively with the hobnailed boots of general moral judgments and pious aphorisms can be as damaging as letting a butcher try his hand at a transplant. Enormous damage can be done through clumsy spiritual direction.

Is it, then, that bishops and provincials have been wise and prudent in not providing regular spiritual direction for the majority of their clergy? Certainly, poor spiritual direction can be a waste of time and even very damaging, but a much greater danger is not to have it at all. Its absence affects not only priests, but above all ordinary people who are still so dependent on priests for spiritual guidance.

Why is it so important to encourage priests to have spiritual direction? Why should it be a first priority in every diocese to ensure that there are suitable people trained as directors? The answer, briefly, is this—in order that the Church may be the Church of Christ and may not lapse into idolatry. It is the most urgent and yet unrecognised need in the Church today.

'That the Church may not lapse into idolatry.' Surely, the Church can never lapse into idolatry, for Christ has promised that the gates of hell shall never prevail against it. And yet shortly after Christ had appointed Peter as the Rock on which the Church was to be built for all time, he foretold his death, and Peter, full of good will and affection for Christ, said, 'This must not happen to you'. Christ turned to him and said, 'Get behind me, Satan. You are an obstacle in my path, because the way you think is not God's way but man's.' (Matthew 16:23) The Gospel hands down this story to be pondered by the future Church. If it was possible for honest, friendly, devoted, courageous Peter to speak with the mind of Satan, there is no reason to suppose that the rest of us—bishops, provincials and priests—should not individually and corporately do the same.

The danger to the Church is not so much that she should suddenly turn into a morally depraved organization, spawning wicked Borgias in the Vatican, but rather that she might succumb to a temptation—the blindness of the scribes and Pharisees. The difficulty about spiritual blindness is that we do not recognise it when we have it. For example, a priest may be a key man within his diocese or Order, most conscientious and hard-working, on every major committee, the builder of many churches, and an obvious candidate for a bishopric, and yet not be a living cell within the Body of Christ. It is not that this key man has abandoned his 'priestly way of life' and is living a life of debauchery on the quiet. He is far too busy for debauchery, is as sober as a judge, as chaste as an angel, as reliable as the diocesan electronic clock, and yet working out of a quite 'worldly' wisdom. St Paul warned the Colossians against an asceticism based on the principles of this world:

> If you have really died with Christ to the principles of this world, why do you still let rules dictate to you, as though you were still living in the world? 'It is forbidden to pick up this, it is forbidden to taste that, it is forbidden to touch something else'; all these prohibitions are only concerned with things which perish by their very use—an example of human doctrines and regulations. It may be argued that true wisdom is to be found in these, with their self-imposed

devotions, their self-abasement and their severe treatment of the body; but once the flesh starts to protest, they are no use at all. (Colossians 2:20–23)

The flesh, for St Paul, means the self which puts its own kingdom before God's Kingdom. That selfish self can easily masquerade as a zealous member of Christ's Kingdom, and the damage is greatest when we begin to deceive ourselves. We have to watch and pray and beg to see beneath the surface of our words and behaviour. For example, statements heard frequently in any policy-making group within the Church which pass as wise and prudent, and may, in fact, be so, can also manifest a loss of faith in Christ's 'seek first the kingdom of God and all these other things will be added to you' (Matthew 6:33). Pleas 'to proceed with caution in this matter' may indicate that fear has become the dominant factor in my life. I shall oppose anything which threatens my security—'speaking with one voice' may mean that the Spirit of truth and justice is no longer the ultimate criterion for our decisions. There are many other examples. And so I can be considered a model priest, a man of wisdom and prudence, and yet I may not be working for Christ's Kingdom but for my own. This is one form of idolatry. Self-idolatry within the Church as a whole may mean that, as it loses touch with the Spirit of Christ, it will become increasingly preoccupied with its own survival. A Church turned in on itself will have little sense of mission, will minister to its own practising members, but will have nothing to say to those who do not belong and will make little effort to do anything for its own lapsed members. Ecumenism will be considered a fringe activity and will be looked on by most as a threat to the Church's survival. There will be little interest in theology, except to condemn those who attempt new formulations of faith in more contemporary language. Faith, having weakened, will no longer seek understanding, but will prefer to rest unthinkingly in the familiar, and justify this attitude by calling it orthodoxy. There will be great emphasis on loyalty and fidelity. Attempts to deepen understanding of the faith and to work out its implications in social and political life will be labelled secularism and condemned. There will be, as Paul says in Galatians (5:20), 'feuds and wrangling within the Church, jealousy, bad temper and quarrels, disagreements, factions and envy'. And yet people will believe that they are still working for the Kingdom of God when, in fact, they are not.

We have elaborated what it means to say that spiritual direction is necessary so that the Church may not lapse into idolatry. There are, however, some more positive reasons to which I would like to turn my attention.

What is it to be a priest? What are the essential qualities required? However we may answer these questions, no one can deny that the most essential and basic quality required in every priest is familiarity with God in prayer. The Church is the sacrament of the living Christ who lives, not in temples made of human hands, but in the minds and hearts of his people. If the Church, body of the living Christ, is not informed by the Spirit who lived in Jesus and raised him from the dead, then she is no longer the Church. 'My ways are not your ways and my thoughts are not your thoughts says the Lord God.' (Isaiah 55:8) Christ's Kingdom is not of this world. The wisdom of God is folly to the world. If the priests of the Church are not attuned to the Spirit, perceptive of it and responsive to it, then they will oppose the Spirit of God. Spiritual direction is about being attuned to the Spirit of the risen Christ, becoming more perceptive and more responsive to him. If it can help us to be so attuned, obviously it is of primary importance.

There is no disagreement in the Church on the need for prayer and on the priest's need of personal prayer. But priests, while not denying the necessity of prayer, find it difficult in practice, become disheartened and, if they do keep up the practice of private prayer, tend to lapse into a mechanical recitation of the breviary or of set prayers, a duty to be done which, like beating your head against a wall, gives a sense of relief when it is over. Many priests are thoroughly confused about the nature of prayer, having had no systematic instruction on how to pray, merely repeated warnings that they must pray if they are to remain true to their vocation. They have picked up snippets of information—for example that the best form of prayer is silent, still, imageless, without thoughts. They make a great effort to be still, to empty the mind of thought and images. The effort seems to activate both mind and imagination. They are tormented with memories, images and thoughts, try to drive them away, become exhausted and emerge from their devotions in a thoroughly bad temper. Others have been told that feelings do not count and should be ignored in prayer (this is still alarmingly common teaching)—so they discount any emotional feelings which arise as mere sentimentality and try to concentrate on making acts of sheer will, an exercise which can leave them feeling very empty and dizzy. Very common is the feeling that they are not good enough to pray and that until they have overcome this or that fault there is no point in trying. This attitude is linked with the most common obstacle of all in prayer; that is, a false image of God. Our notion of God is inevitably formed out of our own experience. Authority as experienced from parents, teachers, superiors inevitably colours our notion of who God is. We may know intellectually that God is not to be identified with the angry parent or the ambitious and heartless headmaster intent only on results. However, the emotional effect of such authority figures and the wounds they have caused in the psyche are still effectively at work deep in our minds, often below our consciousness. They will therefore manifest themselves not in any straightforward manner, but in more devious ways of avoiding any meeting with God, for example, 'I simply do not have time for prayer—am too tired—find God more easily outside prayer'.

Good spiritual direction can free a person of many of these false notions and hang-ups about prayer, can introduce the priest to the infinite variety there is in ways of praying, can encourage him to experiment, teach him methods of praying with his whole person, not just with his mind, and help him to be still so that he can come to know the truth, that is, that there is a sense in which he does not and cannot pray: only the Spirit can pray within him. And the Spirit is the Spirit of God, the God of surprises, the God who is Other, yet nearer to us than we are to ourselves, the God who is present in every event of our lives. Good spiritual direction can help the priest to discover the value in what formerly he termed 'distractions' and to see that the most valuable source of prayer is from within his own memory, for it is in the events of our lives that God is present to us and there is no other way in which we can experience Him. By talking over what he has experienced in prayer time with a spiritual director, without trying to judge or assess the prayer or himself, the priest will become more aware of his inner feelings and begin to notice the qualitative difference in his emotions, recognising some as very superficial and transient, others as deeper and more genuine. This is the beginning of 'discernment of spirits', coming to recognise and distinguish the creative and the destructive movements going on within us and learning how to cooperate with the creative and to grow through the destructive movements by countering them. Learning how to discern the spirits is the first and indispensable step in discovering what God's will is for us in any particular situation. We come to know what is God's will for us by an inner sensing which while not, of course, independent of external criteria, comes from within so that the heart and the feelings know as well as the head. Good spiritual direction can help us to discern our own inner states and through this discernment learn what God's will is for us. The spiritual director helps us to penetrate through the layers of our consciousness and to recognise our blindness and self-deception.

Trahit sua quemque voluptas: 'each one is led by his own desire'. All of us, no matter how docile and obedient we may like to think ourselves, are led by our own desires and we always, in the end, do what we want. It is therefore vitally important that we should discover what we really want. Good spiritual direction can help us to get in touch with this source of our strength, the springs of everlasting life welling up within us.

Spiritual direction is the art of accompanying another person as they explore their experience in prayer. It differs from counselling in that spiritual direction takes place within a context of explicit faith and the immediate subject matter is the person's experience in prayer. The art of the spiritual director is the art of accompanying the other as he enters into his own experience, encouraging him to look at it, articulate the experience and through doing so understand better what is going on. The director's role is to help others discover for themselves, by keeping their attention focused on their own experience, because that is where they will find direction—the presence of the Holy Spirit within their own lives. It is interesting that in the *Spiritual Exercises*, a handbook meant for retreat-givers, St Ignatius does not speak of retreat directors but of 'the giver of the Exercises'. He presumes that the director is the Holy Spirit.

If priests had a better knowledge of the purpose of spiritual direction, they would be less reluctant to look for it. The more common notion of a spiritual director is of someone with penetrating eyes who can read souls (that is, know their vices and weaknesses) without having to listen to them and can then give perceptive and sound advice for the correction of their lives in the future. There are people who have this gift of seeing. Unless their vision is distorted they see the whole person, not merely the faults, and therefore see them as precious and loveable. But however accurate and penetrating their insights may be, they can do the others no good unless they can enable them to see for themselves, for it is only when this happens that any inner transformation can take place. Otherwise the effect of the far-seeing director may be to leave the person more guilt-ridden, and therefore less capable of acting differently, than before.

The most essential element in spiritual direction is the trust that is built up between the director and the other. The relationship must be one of equality and the director must in no way sit in judgment on the other. That is why the old Celtic name 'soul friend', or that French *accompagnateur* are preferable to 'director'. In this atmosphere of trust a person can enter his or her own consciousness and begin to learn more profoundly who God is. Unless there is an atmosphere of great trust, people will not dare to enter the dark areas of their own experience, but will do their best to ignore them or run away from them. Unfortunately (or fortunately, as it turns out) these dark areas will not leave us. Entering into them through prayer (meditating on sin) can be a most liberating experience, freeing us from fear, revealing to us the astonishing goodness of God who has not run away from our darkness, but entered into it and redeemed it. In the light and inner knowledge of his goodness, we can begin to see more clearly the deceptions which have been operative in us. Knowing his love and forgiveness, we do not have to be on the defensive any more or cling to false securities.

Once the priest is more at home with God in prayer, he will be more at home with himself and more at home with his people. He will experience an at-one-ness and become free of any damaging strain between his role as a priest and his being a person. He will not have to pretend or put on airs or constantly be looking over his shoulder. In Christ he will be moving to an ever greater freedom, better able to understand what is going on in his people because he has been able to enter into his own experience and has discovered that God is at work in all things, and that there is no human experience, even if it includes damage done to us by others, or damage to ourselves by our own sins, which God cannot use to draw us to Himself.

From my own experience as a priest, and especially during the last seven years when I have given individual retreats to hundreds of people—priests, religious and laity, and across a mixture of Christian denominations—I know that there is no shortage of men and women in the Church, a very high proportion of them laity, who are familiar with God in prayer, have a good self-knowledge, sound spiritual judgment and an ability to enter into another person's experience and to accompany them unobtrusively. They could, if they were able to find the time and money for training, perform a most important and necessary ministry in the Church. I hope that this article may encourage bishops and religious superiors to recommend and finance some of their people to undergo such training.

On Being an Adult in Today's Church

JESUS SAID, 'Unless you become as little children you cannot enter the Kingdom of heaven' (Matthew 18:3), so one essential characteristic of adults in the Church is that they should be like little children!

If you feel uneasy at this opening sentence, I share your unease, for the Church, as we experience it in Britain today, is still too paternalistic, a 'Father Church' rather than the 'Mother Church' of which liturgy speaks, very protective of his little ones, ensuring they are provided with a good Catholic education and reserving a large part of his slender income for this purpose. Father does quite well with his infants, but cannot cope with his stroppy adolescent sons and daughters, and is no longer on speaking terms with many of his grown-up children. He is desperately anxious to have them back, and is pained and baffled by their refusal to return. He is convinced, however, that the home must be kept in order and the rules of the family, which he lays down, must be observed, lest the little ones, and those grown-up members who are still at home and have remained little ones, whom he fondly refers to as 'the simple faithful', should be scandalized.

David, who was three years old at the time, handed me a book, pointed to a story and asked me to read it to him at bedtime. It was a long story including, as I thought, ideas and words too complex for an infant, so I omitted the occasional sentence and simplified some words. Every slightest deviation from the text was corrected by the illiterate David lying back on his pillow. When I reached 'happily ever after', he was quite huffy and critical of my performance.

Infants are naturally conservative and lovers of set ritual, rarely tiring of doing and saying the same thing again and again. They take great delight in long words, in nonsensical rhymes, loving the sounds but not yet interested in the meaning. Perhaps the reason is that familiar sounds, sights and gestures answer a deep need, the need to feel safe, secure and protected. Infants are still recovering from the traumatic experience of birth when they were expelled from the warmth and security of the womb into a completely new world of sights, sounds and pains from which they are no longer so protected, therefore they cling to whatever gives security, whether it be mother, father, a rag doll or, like Linus, a piece of blanket. The process of growing up is a learning not to cling, a gradual letting go of those securities which, if I continue to cling to them, stifle my life.

The growing process can be pictured in a series of concentric circles, beginning with the first circle, life in the womb. After a nine-month period we are ready to emerge into the next circle of home, where we need another incubation period of care, protection and affection to build up strength to face the wider circle of life at school and in the immediate neighbourhood. Readers can describe these circles for themselves—home, locality, job, perhaps university, county, country, nationality, religious affiliation, ideology etc., and each stage of growth requires a shorter or longer period of incubation before we are ready and strong enough to move into a wider circle of life and experience.

It is not wrong to cling to our securities: self-preservation is our most basic and strongest instinct, and without it we should perish at birth. We need to cling to our securities in order to build up our inner strength to face the next circle of life and experience. The danger is that we become so attached to the security provided in any one circle that we dare not proceed any further. We can become like fat caterpillars safely clinging to our cabbage leaf. We see our caterpillar friends behaving oddly and beginning to disintegrate. We resolve to keep our many feet firmly on the cabbage leaf and begin to develop a hard carapace to ensure that nothing odd happens to us. We die without knowing our real identity, our freedom and our glory.

As human beings, what is our real identity, our freedom and our glory? The pagan poet Terence, who lived before Christ, was groping for an answer when he wrote *'Homo sum: humani nil a me alienum puto'*, 'I am a human being: I consider nothing that is human to be foreign to me'. Terence, if his poetry was a self-expression, had reached adulthood, was no longer parochial, narrowly nationalist, racist, sexist, militarist. The sky was the roof of his home and the earth his hearth: he was at home in creation.

St Paul reveals the answer for which Terence was searching.

> Life to me, of course, is Christ, but then death would bring me something more. (Philippians 1:21)

> In him [Christ] were created all things in heaven and on earth—all things were created through him and for him …. because God wanted all perfection to be found in him and all things to be reconciled through him and for him, everything in heaven and everything on earth, when he made peace by his death on the cross. (Colossians 1:16, 19–20)

> You must live your whole life according to the Christ you have received—Jesus the Lord; you must be rooted in him and built on him—make sure that no one traps you and deprives you of your freedom by some second-hand, empty, rational philosophy based on the principles of this world instead of on Christ. (Colossians 2:6–8)

Our true identity is in Christ with the Father, in whom all creation has its being. Our glory is in having the strength,

> … to grasp the breadth and the length, the height and the depth, until knowing the love of Christ, which is beyond all knowledge, we are filled with the utter fullness of God— whose power, working in us, can do infinitely more than we can think or imagine. (Ephesians 3:18–20)

Becoming an adult in the Church is to learn to be at home, not just within my own family, circle, region, country or nation, or within my own stereotypes, but to be at home in God, who is in all things. Christian teaching about the need for detachment is teaching about being adult in the Church and in the world, is about being at home and free in both, so that we can find our true identity, to be at one with Christ.

We cannot be at home in the Church and in the world unless we feel safe and secure in them, for both Church and world are very frightening. Our ability to let go our familiar securities and grow into ever-widening circles of life depends upon our ability to trust. That is why a childlike trust in the all-pervading goodness and protection of God is essential if we are to become adult in the Church and in society. If we trust in God's loving care in all things and in all circumstances, then we can afford to explore life, take risks. Being liberated from fear, we have no need to be constantly defensive and no desire to live our lives within the confines of a narrow cocoon, whether it be of our own or of someone else's making.

It is childlike trust which enables us to become adult. Being intelligent and academically well qualified does not necessarily save us from remaining infantile. In fact, intellectual gifts may enable us to build a narrower and tougher cocoon around ourselves than a less intelligent person could construct, for intelligent people can argue more convincingly in favour of their prejudices, hiding their timidity behind awesome phrases about standing by their principles and having the courage of their convictions, quoting selectively from the writings of the famous in support of their position, disguising their cowardice with the name of prudence and claiming their inability to say or do anything authentic to be evidence of their humility and obedience. Illiterate, uneducated, simple people, who have faith in God present in all things, can be very adult members of the Church and of society, because they move through the complexity and pain of life with a peace and serenity which no one can take from them, are interested in all they encounter, are not at all ashamed of their poverty or ignorance but are always open and ready to learn.

On Being an Adult in Today's Church

Our growth through infancy to adulthood may be compared to a mountain climb. Adulthood does not represent the summit, but rather the final stage of the climb, which may be much steeper, more arduous and dangerous than anything we encountered in earlier stages. On the lower slopes, in infancy and adolescence, we need to be given precise instruction, and sometimes have to be carried, supported with rails and ladders. In the adult stage of the climb we become responsible for our own route and direction. It would be very odd behaviour in climbers who had reached the adult stage if they were continually grumbling that instructors are still shouting precise instructions to the infants and adolescents on the lower slopes. When we complain about paternalism and clericalism in the Church, it can be a sign of our own failure to reach adulthood. More justified are the complaints of those adults who find that their guides will not allow them to begin the adult stage of their climb, but insist on still treating them as though they were infants. Such complaints are widespread and suggest that the guides themselves may never have experienced the adult stage, do not know how to proceed there, and prefer to keep all climbers on the lower slopes, securely roped and limited to familiar, well-trod routes, assuring any who deviate from their instructions that they will certainly fall to their death.

A current indication of the Church's failure to reach adulthood is the present Fleet Street newspapers' reaction to the Bishop of Durham's habit of emphasizing neglected aspects of Christian doctrine by his use of startling phrases, 'the Resurrection is not a conjuring trick with old bones', etc., causing indignation and anger in a nation not normally interested in theology, and causing still fiercer anger when he dares to apply Christian teaching to some of the political and social structures in which we choose to live.[1]

---

[1] David Jenkins, the Anglican bishop of Durham from 1984 to 1994, made this widely misinterpreted comment in a radio interview on *Poles Apart* (BBC Radio 4, October 1984). *Ed.*

The public reaction to Bishop Jenkins is like the three-year-old David's reaction to my abridged and amended account of his favourite fairy story. The meaning of these doctrines is of no great interest: what is essential is that they should sound right.

Christian doctrine is given to us as a light for our darkness. A child, terrified of the dark and with no intention of exploring it, may become very attached to a particular torch, its taste, texture, shape, and will enjoy turning it on and off in a well-lit room. The child may become so attached to the torch that it becomes his constant companion, an attachment which may continue even when the torch is broken beyond repair. It has become a symbol of security for the child. If anyone should try to take it away or substitute another, there will be hell to pay and the evildoer will be delated to mother or father.

In the Church we can be like this fretful child in our attitude to doctrine, no longer using it to shed light on the darkness of our world, but cherishing its textual form as though it were a good in itself, creating a rumpus if anyone should question the form in which we learnt the doctrine as children and reporting to ecclesiastical authorities anyone who seems to tamper with it. We may also find an additional security in the doctrine in that we hold it, while most people do not. This attitude can masquerade as orthodoxy: in fact it is infantilism, a cocooning of our minds against the risk of uncertainty.

Our church vocabulary reflects this childish attitude. We talk of 'the deposit of faith' as though it were an object best kept in a bank vault, so we speak of 'preserving the faith', 'defending the faith'. In popular understanding, faith comes to mean asserting as true a series of propositions which, being mysteries, are beyond our understanding and therefore best left alone. Such an understanding of faith can become an effectively narrow cocoon protecting us from truth, a Christless attitude which may have nothing to do with a love relationship with the Lord of all creation.

The most serious indication of our failure to be adult in the Church can be seen in our misunderstanding and misuse of authority. The Latin root of the word 'obedience' is *obaudire*, which means 'to listen to attentively'. The object of our listening is God. The Latin root of the word 'authority' is *augeo*, meaning 'I increase, I grow'. The function of authority in the Church is to help us to grow, to become adult, so that we may become more perceptive and responsive to the mysterious action of God in every detail of our lives; and the action of God is unique to each individual. Any exercise of authority in the Church which is so rigid that it undermines people's confidence in their own experience, making them afraid to listen to the promptings of the Spirit within their own hearts, is a serious misuse of authority, alienating people from their inner selves and so cutting them off from the Spirit of God at work in their spirit. There can be no greater danger than this in the Church, because misunderstanding and misuse of authority can lead us into idolatry, the substitution of a creature for the Creator.

One indication of infantilism in those in authority is their rigidity. Because they are afraid and cannot face their own darkness and weakness, they become very intolerant of those weaknesses in their subjects and so punish them severely. Children learn through their mistakes, and wise parents are tolerant. If a child learning to walk is scolded every time it falls, the child will never learn to walk. If, in the Church, the adult laity, deprived of responsibility, are suddenly given it, they are bound to make many mistakes at first. Adult authority will be able to bear this chaos and uncertainty, and will trust people's learning ability. Infants in authority are tyrants, and cannot endure any deviation from what is familiar to them.

Immaturity, both in the exercise of authority and in unquestioning subjection to it, is widespread in the Church in my experience. Recently I wrote an article for Pax Christi's periodical *Justpeace*, in which I expressed my interest in working on spirituality with laypeople who are active in peace and justice work. I have had many replies welcoming this initiative, but adding that little or no encouragement is given to active peace work in the local parish and that it is unlikely that a peace group would be allowed to use the local parish for a retreat on peace spirituality! Why this nervousness about the peace issue? The Catholic Church is easily roused to action on matters of sexual morality, while remaining apathetic on wider issues, e.g. human rights, violence, nuclear war, in spite of excellent social encyclicals of recent popes. It is good that the Church does speak on the abortion issue, but strange that the underlying principle, namely the sacredness of human life, is not so vigorously applied to life outside the womb. Could it be that this preoccupation with contraception and abortion, an obsession with the womb, is reflecting the truth that we are still in our infancy and have not yet broken through to adolescence and adulthood?

One group of people who suffer today from the immaturity of the Church are those men and women who marry across the religious denominations. God brings them together in love, but His priests and ministers usually become very nervous at this divine action and so they, sometimes together with the families of such a couple, try to persuade them to avoid taking such a risk. Fortunately, many couples persist. In loving one another, they are doing God's will, and when they marry they live out an ecumenism which, the Catholic Church says, should be a priority in all our ministry. The clergy, however, become very nervous when the couple want to attend one another's services, to bring up their children to be familiar with both Churches, to celebrate the baptism of their children into Christ's Church in a joint service for both denominations, to receive the Eucharist together in both Churches. Immature exercise of authority will always try to make things as difficult as possible for such couples, and they may be brow-beaten with what is presented as theological argument, in which they feel lost and incompetent. Because the couple's own understanding of authority is probably also immature, therefore they feel confused, hurt and scandalized. In a more adult

Church, such couples would be encouraged to live in unity across their denominations, assured that such harmony is God's will for them and that their experience is of value to the Church. Similarly, too, the divorced and separated should be listened to carefully, for they have much to teach the Church about marriage, its nature, how to prepare for it, etc., rather than be treated as though they were delinquent children who can only cause mischief in the Church.

Today there is such nervousness in church authorities over those Christians who, while believing in law and committed to its observance, have a more adult understanding of the meaning and purpose of law than their pastors, and therefore feel bound in conscience deliberately to break those laws of the land which are unjust. To insist that all the laws of the land are sacrosanct is infantile, idolatrous and highly dangerous. To have damaged the gas chambers in which Jews were to be murdered in Nazi Germany would have been considered a criminal offence at the time; today we would look on such an offence as heroism. To chain oneself to the Ministry of Defence buildings, or to cut the barbed wire at Greenham or Molesworth is to break the law of the land, yet Greenham at present, and Molesworth shortly, contain flying ovens for the incineration of unknown citizens and we, as a nation, do not have control over their use.[2] The Church must uphold law and order, and her members are bound to render to Caesar what is Caesar's. But the Church must be equally clear about rendering to God what is God's, otherwise she is colluding in idolatry.

I hope these examples of immaturity in the Church have not depressed the reader! Restlessness and opposition to domineering parents, however well intentioned the parents may be, is a sign of healthy growth in adolescents. It is only when we begin to grow up that we also begin to recognise our own immaturity, so the examples

---

[2] This refers to peace protests, including civil disobedience, at the sites of US nuclear cruise missiles located on British soil but under US control. *Ed.*

given of immaturity in the Church are also examples of growth. If the process of growth is to continue, what is most needed?

I think that the first requirement is that more responsibility should be given to the laity. Any one person's experience is very limited, but I have met many other people who share my experience, especially through individual retreat-giving, that there is a wealth of wisdom and spiritual experience among the laity in the Church, but no effective means of communicating it. A few years ago there was a National Pastoral Congress held in Liverpool, and attended by two thousand lay delegates from England and Wales. The Congress showed that the Catholic family is very alive, healthy and kicking responsibly, but the parents got cold feet, muffled the laity reports in their response, 'The Easter People', and the most committed members of the Church became the most disheartened. The bishops and clergy must be more adult in their exercise of authority, showing more trust in the action of the Holy Spirit, bond of our unity, and less in regulations.

The second requirement is prayer, because it is in prayer principally, although not exclusively, that we come to know, with an inner knowing, the love of God operating in every detail of our lives and in every particle of creation. It is in the strength of this inner knowing that we can dare to break through the barriers of selfish self-preservation. If we do not break through our fear barriers, for example, currently projected on to the Soviet Union, our barriers, expressed in nuclear arms, will destroy the world, sacrament of God's presence. Help in prayer and spiritual guidance is the most urgent need in the Church today. Without it we shall remain infantile and dangerous.

Gerard W. Hughes: A Bibliography

Books

In Search of a Way: Two Journeys of Spiritual Discovery. Rome and Sydney: E. J. Dwyer, 1978; New York: Image Books, 1980; edn 2, London: Darton, Longman and Todd, 1986.

God of Surprises. London: Darton, Longman and Todd, 1985; edn 2, with new preface, 1996; translations into French (1987), Swedish (1994), Polish (1996), Japanese (1997), German (1998), Finnish (2005), Chinese (2006), Slovak (2006) and Spanish (2012).

Prayer and Peace Action. London: Fellowship of Reconciliation, 1986 (pamphlet).

Letting the Word Become Flesh: Daily Readings and Reflections for Advent. London: Pax Christi, 1988.

Show Me Your Face: Daily Readings and Reflections for Lent. London: Pax Christi, 1990.

Walk to Jerusalem in Search of Peace. London: Darton, Longman and Todd, 1991; translation into Finnish (2014).

What's Your God Like? Ropley: Hunt and Thorpe, 1991 (short booklet); translations into Finnish (1995) and French (2007).

O God Why? Journey through Lent for Bruised Pilgrims. Oxford: Bible Reading Fellowship, 1993; new edn, 1996 (subtitle, *A Spiritual Journey Towards Meaning, Wisdom and Strength*); translations into Swedish (2001) and Finnish (2008).

(with Joyce Huggett and others), *Day by Day: Bible Readings for Every Day of the Year*, volumes 2 and 3. Oxford: Bible Reading Fellowship, 1994, 1995.

(with Sheila Cassidy and others) *Triumph of Hope: Reflections on the Scripture Readings for Lent*. London: CAFOD, 1996.

(with Sheila Cassidy and others), *Your Kingdom Come*. London: Darton, Longman and Todd, 1997.

God, Where are You? London: Darton, Longman and Todd, 1997.

God of Compassion. London: Hodder and Stoughton, 1998.

Seven Weeks for the Soul: A Reflective Journey for Lent or Other Times of Renewal. Chicago: Loyola, 2000.

God in All Things. London, Hodder and Stoughton, 2003; translations into Norwegian (2003), Swedish (2004), Danish (2006) and Korean (2009).

Cry of Wonder. London: Bloomsbury, 2014.

At Home in God: Essays from The Way, *1962–1985*. Oxford: Way Books, 2015 (reprinted articles).

Book Articles and Introductions

'God in All Things', in Patrick Barry, *Prayer in Practice*. London: Catholic Truth Society, 1986.

'Foreword', in Francis Dewar, *Live for a Change: Discovering and Using Your Gifts*. London: Darton, Longman and Todd, 1988.

'Foreword', in Anne Long, *Listening*. London: Darton, Longman and Todd, 1990.

'Foreword' in Marion Morgan, *Pilgrims' Guide to the Kingdom*. Bristol: Shoreline, 1990.

'Introduction', in Ursula Burton, *Vicky: A Bridge between Two Worlds*. London: Darton, Longman and Todd, 1991.

'El uso y la trascendencia de las criaturas en una civilización de abundancia o carencia', in *Ejercicios espirituales y mundo de hoy*, edited by Juan Manuel García-Lomas. Bilbao and Santander: Mensajero and Sal Terrae, 1992.

'Foreword', in Cyril Ashton, *Threshold God: Discovering Christ in the Margins of Life*. London: Darton, Longman and Todd, 1992.

'Foreword', in Dorothy Fielding, *Descent into Light*. London: Burns and Oates, 1994.

'Foreword', in Susan Hardwick, *A Weaving of Peace*. Bury St Edmunds: Kevin Mayhew, 1996.

'Praying through Silence', in *Pathways of Prayer*, edited by Graham Dow. London: Darton, Longman and Todd, 1997.

'Foreword', in Peter Tyler *The Way of Ecstasy: Praying with Teresa of Avila*. Norwich: Canterbury, 1997.

'A Spirituality for Christians in Public Life', in *Changing World, Unchanging Church?*, edited by David Clark. London: Mowbray, 1997.

'Foreword', in Margaret Silf, *Landmarks: Exploration of Ignatian Spirituality*. London: Darton, Longman and Todd, 1998 (US edn published as *Inner Compass*).

'Henri J. M. Nouwen—A Personal Appreciation', in Henri Nouwen, *Reaching Out*, new edn. London: Fount, 1998.

'Unity in Prayer', in *For God's Sake, Unity: An Ecumenical Voyage with the Iona Community*, edited by Maxwell Craig. Glasgow: Wild Goose, 1998.

'Is There a Spirituality for the Elderly? An Ignatian Approach', in *Spirituality and Ageing*, edited by Albert Jewell. London: Jessica Kingsley, 1999.

'Preface', in Peter McVerry, *Jesus: Social Revolutionary?* Dublin: Veritas, 1999.

'Foreword', in Barbara Butler and Jo White, *To Be a Pilgrim: A Comprehensive Guide*. Stowmarket: Kevin Mayhew, 2002.

'Foreword to the New Edition', in Donald Nicholl, *Holiness*. London: Darton, Longman and Todd, 2004.

'Introduction', in *The Spiritual Exercises of Saint Ignatius of Loyola*, translated by Michael Ivens. Leominster: Gracewing, 2004.

'Foreword', in Gerald O'Mahony, *A Way in to the Trinity: The Story of a Journey*. Leominster: Gracewing, 2004.

'Foreword', in Michael Mayne, *The Enduring Melody*. London: Darton, Longman and Todd, 2006.

'Funeral Homily', in Michael Ivens, *Keeping in Touch: Posthumous Papers on Ignatian Topics*. Leominster: Gracewing, 2007.

'Guidelines for Distinguishing the Creative from the Destructive', in Anita M. Woodwell, *On Holy Ground: Guided Prayer: A Handbook and Practical Companion*. Norwich: Canterbuty, 2008.

'Ignatian Spirituality', in *The Bloomsbury Guide to Christian Spirituality*, edited by Peter Tyler and Richard Woods. London: Bloomsbury, 2012.

Journal Articles and Reviews

'German Protestants and the Coming Council', *The Tablet*, 19 September 1959, 780–781.

'Renouncing the World', *The Way*, 2/1, January 1962, 44–51.

'Divine Providence and Germany's Tragedy', *Clergy Review*, 45, 1960, 214–224.

'Campus Ministry', *The Way Supplement*, 22, Summer 1974, 78–84.

'The First Week and the Formation of Conscience', *The Way Supplement*, 24, Spring 1975, 6–14.

'Footing It to Rome', *The Tablet*, 16 August 1975, 766–767; 23 August 1975, 791–792; 30 August 1975, 815–816; 6 September 1975, 838–839; 13 September 1975, 864.

'Dying We Live', *The Way*, 16/2, April 1976, 114–123.

'Forgotten Truths of the Spiritual Exercises', *The Way Supplement*, 27 (Spring 1976), 69–78; reprinted in *The Way of Ignatius Loyola*, edited by Philip Sheldrake, London: SPCK, 1991.

Review of Alan Ecclestone, *Yes to God*, in *The Month*, May 1976, 283.

'Jesuit Schools and the Apostolate to the Unbeliever', *The Way Supplement*, 31, Summer 1977, 47–55.

'Formation for Freedom', *The Way Supplement*, 32, Autumn 1977, 38–46.

'Spiritual Development: I. An Analysis: II. Pastoral Practice', *Clergy Review*, 65, 1980, 177–181; 215–221.

'Spiritual Development and the Directed Retreat', *The Way Supplement*, 38, Summer 1980, 6–17.

'Four Unilateralists', *The Tablet*, 4 June 1983, 520–521 (followed by extensive correspondence in subsequent issues).

'Spiritual Direction and the Priest', *The Way Supplement*, 47, Summer 1983, 26–33.

'On Being an Adult in Today's Church', *The Way*, 25/4, October 1985, 259–266.

'Peace Spirituality', *Julian Meetings Magazine*, 1986; reprinted in *Circles of Silence*, edited by Robert Llewelyn. London: Darton, Longman and Todd, 1994.

'The Spirituality of Peace', *The Month*, April 1987, 155–158.

'Walking to Jerusalem', *The Tablet*, 18 April 1987, 420–422; 2 May 1987, 454–458; 30 May 1987, 570–572; 20 June 1987, 654–656; 4 July 1987, 715–716.

Review of George Weigel, *Tranquillitas Ordinis*, Roger Ruston, *A Say in the End of the World* and James O'Connell, *Notes towards a Theology of Peace*, in *The Month*, February 1990, 72–73.

Review of *The Writings of Daniel Berrigan*, in *The Tablet*, 11 August 1990, 1018.

'New Ways of Encounter', *The Tablet*, 25 August 1990, 1070–1071.

'A Chaplain Reflects', *The Tablet*, 6 October 1990, 1274–1275.

'Sheep of War or Dog of Faith?', *The Month*, December 1991, 176, 222.

'The Poor Man's Mysticism', *The Tablet*, 9 March 1991, 298–299.

Bibliography

'Our Inner Wealth', *The Tablet*, 17 August 1991, 993–995.

'Shades of the Ghetto', *The Tablet*, 7 November 1992, 1396–1397.

'The Battle of St Philip's', *The Tablet*, 12 December 1992, 1572 (letter to the editor).

Review of A. N. Wilson, *Jesus*, in *The Month*, January 1993, 30.

Review of D. E. Harding, *The Trial of the Man Who Said He Was God*, in *The Month*, February 1993, 77.

New Daylight (22 May – 4 June 1994).

'Parables of the Spirit', *The Tablet*, 8 October 1994, 1262–1263.

Review of Sara Maitland, *A Big Enough God*, in *The Tablet*, 7 January 1995, 20.

'Retreat for MPs and Others at Westminster', *Letters and Notices*, 1995, 233–234.

'Are You a Spiritual Person?', *Mount Carmel*, 43/3, October 1995, 5.

'L'utilisation et la transcendance des choses crées dans un monde d'abondance et de misère', *Cahiers de Spiritualité Ignatienne*, 82, 1997.

'Be Still and Know', *The Tablet*, 23 August 1997, 1067–1068.

'Knocking on Heaven's Door', *The Tablet*, 21 February 1998, 247–248.

'Holy Disobedience', *The Tablet*, 5 September 1998, 1143–1144.

'Finding Life by Losing It', *The Tablet*, 18 December 1999, 1709–1710.

'Listen to the Music', *The Tablet*, 22 January 2000, 78.

'Free to Find Our Deepest Desire', *The Tablet*, 24 June 2000, 856–857; Dutch translation, 'Vrij zijn om te vinden wat wij ten diepste verlangen', *Cardoner*, 20, 2001, 49–56.

'Following the Magi', *The Tablet*, 23 December 2000, 1739–1740.

'The Enigma of the Smiling Crucifix', *The Tablet*, 26 March 2005, 4–5.

'Advent Reflections', *The Tablet*, 26 November 2005, 17; 3 December 2005, 23; 10 December 2005, 10; 17 December 2005, 20.

'The Real Meaning of Deterrence', *The Tablet*, 22 April 2006, 6–7; reprinted in *Tui Motu Interislands*, June 2006, 13–14.

'Allowing Ourselves to be Disturbed', *Ground Zero*, 11/4, October 2006, 6–7.

'Lenten Reflections', *The Tablet*, 24 February 2007, 15; 3 March 2007, 9; 10 March 2007; 24 March 2007, 14; 31 March 2007, 11; 7 April 2007, 12.

'The Conversion of St Paul', *Thinking Faith*, 25 January 2008.

'Neglecting the Real Eucharistic Presence?', *Pastoral Review*, 4/5, September–October 2008.

'To Whom May the Spiritual Exercises Be Given?', *Letters and Notices*, 2011, 293–292.

'A Spark from the Kirk in Crichton', *Pastoral Review*, 8/2, March–April 2012.

Interview with Brendan Walsh, *The Tablet*, 25 October 2014.